P9-BYV-587

REMODEL
PLUMBING

REMODEL
PLUMBING

REX CAULDWELL

SOUTH HUNTINGTON
PUBLIC LIBRARY
HUNTINGTON STATION

The Taunton Press

696.1
Cau

Text © 2005 by Rex Cauldwell

Photographs © 2005 by Rex Cauldwell, except p. 51 top right courtesy of Vanguard Piping Systems, www.vanguardpipe.com; p. 100 courtesy of Oregon Copper Bowl Company, www.OCBC.net; p. 144 right courtesy of American Standard, www.americanstandard-us.com

Illustrations © 2005 by The Taunton Press, Inc.

All rights reserved.

The Taunton Press
Inspiration for hands-on living®

The Taunton Press, Inc., 63 South Main Street, PO Box 5506, Newtown, CT 06470-5506

e-mail: tp@taunton.com

Editor: Steve Cory
Interior design: Jeff Potter/Potter Publishing Studio
Layout: Susan Fazekas
Illustrator: Chuck Lockhart
Photographer: Rex Cauldwell

For Pros/by Pros® is a trademark of The Taunton Press, Inc., registered in the U.S. Patent and Trademark Office.

Library of Congress Cataloging-in-Publication Data
Cauldwell, Rex.
  Remodel plumbing / Rex Cauldwell.
    p. cm. -- (For pros, by pros)
  Includes index.
  ISBN 1-56158-698-6
  1. Plumbing--Amateurs' manuals. 2. Dwellings--Remodeling--Amateurs' manuals. I. Title. II. Series.
  TH6124.C38 2005
  696'.1--dc22

                        2004022366

Printed in the United States of America
10 9 8 7 6 5 4 3 2 1

The following manufacturers/names appearing in *Remodel Plumbing* are trademarks:
American Standard®, Apollo®, Champion®, Corian®, Dawn®, DeWalt®, Eljer®, Fernco®, Fiberglas®, Flowguard Gold®, In-Sink-Erator®, Jacuzzi®, Karran®, Kohler®, Lasco®, LSP®, Makita®, Oatey®, Oregon Copper Bowl®, Qwik Jon®, Rubbermaid®, Safe Flo®, Studor®, Swanstone®, Teflon®, Thompson™, Plastics, Inc., Vanguard®, Vaseline®, Velcro®, Zoeller Co.®

About Your Safety: Plumbing is inherently dangerous. We try to promote safe work practices throughout this book, but what is safe for one builder or homeowner under certain circumstances may not be safe for you under different circumstances. So don't try anything you learn about here (or elsewhere) unless you're certain that it's safe for you. If something doesn't feel right, don't do it. Look for another way. Please keep safety foremost in your mind whenever you're working.

To my two grandchildren, Katy and Elizabeth

ACKNOWLEDGMENTS

I would like to thank the following people and manufacturers for providing products and information for this book. In addition, I would like to thank my most ardent fan, Carl, for all his ideas and input about the trades.

American Standard (Nora DePalma of Building Products, Inc. for American Standard), 800-442-1902 (www.american-standard-us.com); In-Sink-Erator (Elaine Wills), 800-558-5700 (www.insinkerator. com); Oatey Products (Marti Stalinski), 800-203-1155; Oregon Copper Bowl Company (Lance Hull), 541-485-9845 (www.OCBC.net); Sioux Chief Manufacturing, 800-821-3944 (www.siouxchief. com); Studor, Inc., 800-447-4721 (www. studor.com); Thompson Plastics, Inc., 800-272-2782 (www.cpvc.com); Vanguard Piping Systems, Inc. (www. vanguardpipe.com); Zoe Industries, 888-287-1757 (www.showerbuddy.com); Zoeller Pump Company (Tony Renfro), 800-928-7867 (www.zoeller.com).

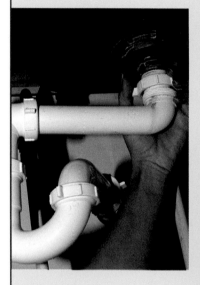

Contents

Introduction

I am a third-generation plumber. I learned the trade from my uncle Bud, who in turn was taught by his father. I remember Uncle Bud telling me that I should be paying him for all the experience I was getting (at that time I was making 25¢ cents an hour). And he was right.

Remodeling work requires a special kind of thinking. When I was working with Uncle Bud, he taught me to think ahead and figure out what problems he was going to encounter so that I could have a specific tool waiting for him when he needed it. I was to plop the tool in his hand without him asking for it. Though I didn't know it then, such thinking was to become an invaluable aid when I became a master plumber doing my own remodeling work.

In remodeling work, there is no straight-line thinking. Simply put, things normally do not work out as originally planned. You never know what you will come across, and you have to be able to work around problems. Throughout this book, I've presented problems and then given solutions to help you create, within

yourself, a logical thinking procedure that can pull you through when you come across a tricky situation.

Many books cover only copper or just plastic. Not so here. This book treats the complete range of water supply lines you will likely encounter on a remodel job: galvanized, copper, PB, CPVC, and PEX. You will learn not just how to install them but how to tie them into an existing system.

Many times I am asked which pipe is best. I will not tell you which is best because, if installed properly, any pipe system will work just fine. Instead, I list all the advantages and disadvantages of each type so you can make up your own mind. I also show you how to work with these types of pipes, illustrating shortcuts and tools you may not know about. And then I show you how to interface the pipe into different sorts of plumbing pipe systems. I cover drain lines extensively, showing you how to install new lines and tie into old systems.

Once you've digested all there is to know about pipe and fittings, I focus on actual remodel jobs. These are not projects created in a showroom or just for a photo shoot. These are actual plumbing remodel projects. From these real-life work situations, you'll gain knowledge and experience that you can take to your job to get it done faster and better.

Who needs this book? Anyone, pro or novice, who does plumbing work. If you are doing a plumbing job, whether brand new or a simple add-on, it is always a good idea to know all about the different types of pipe, their advantages and disadvantages, and to have a stockpile of a variety of solutions that have come down the pike. And this book doesn't provide just my own solutions and knowledge but that from two generations previous, passed along from my uncle and grandfather. Take this information, add to it, and share it with me in an e-mail (ltmtnele@yahoo.com). I would love to hear from you.

CHAPTER 1

The Water Supply System

A FRIEND OF MINE had just replaced the water supply pipes in his house. (We technical people call these pipes the water distribution system.) As his wife took the first shower, he turned on the sink faucet to wash his hands. Her scream announced that all was not well with his design—her hot shower had just turned ice cold. He learned the importance of a properly designed water distribution system, and I got a new customer. A well-designed water distribution system doesn't just deliver water to the points of need. It also delivers reasonably constant water temperature and pressure. Such a system will not only promote harmony between spouses but will also serve as a selling point when the home is on the market.

In this chapter, I show you how to design and install the two most common water distribution systems and a system of my own design. I also describe installation aids, common problems, and solutions. Last, I discuss how to design a system that keeps the water quiet: No more rushing-water noise in the walls or hammer noise coming from the pipes when someone turns off the faucet.

A well-designed water supply system can deliver a good high-power spray in the shower; a poor one, only a dribble.

How Water Gets Routed through a House

Before you start working with a house's water lines, you need to know three things: First, how to recognize a poorly designed system so you won't be surprised with added problems down the road. Second, how to design and install a proper system. And last, what part of the water line to tee into when adding on. Teeing into a poorly designed system or teeing in at the wrong place in a well-designed system can lead to major problems.

The Series System

The series system is the one we see most often. This design attempts to give the best water distribution for the money using just one main feed. Because there is only one main feed, you will have to put

Design Rules

- Drain and vent lines have priority over water lines. Run all drain and vent lines first.
- Keep water lines out of the outside wall in climates that freeze. Instead, run lines up through the floor (or under the slab) to get to the fixture.
- All shutoff valves in the main water line, and taps to fixtures, hot or cold, should be ball valves.
- All under-sink shutoff valves (aka stop valves or fixture shutoff valves) should also be ball valves (quarter turn). The common valves that are usually installed under the fixture have a habit of sticking and leaking (see "Ball Valves Are Best," on p. 17).

Well-Designed Series System

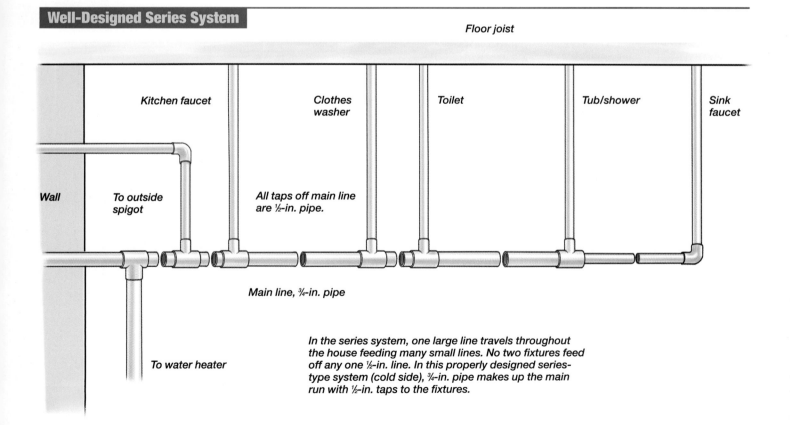

Floor joist

Kitchen faucet

Clothes washer

Toilet

Tub/shower

Sink faucet

Wall

To outside spigot

All taps off main line are ½-in. pipe.

Main line, ¾-in. pipe

To water heater

In the series system, one large line travels throughout the house feeding many small lines. No two fixtures feed off any one ½-in. line. In this properly designed series-type system (cold side), ¾-in. pipe makes up the main run with ½-in. taps to the fixtures.

Poorly Designed Series System

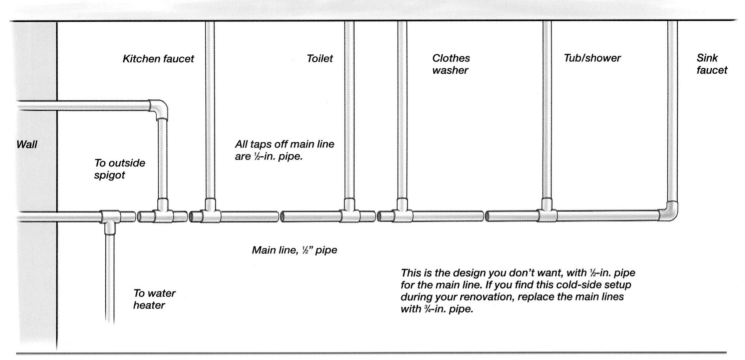

Floor joist

Kitchen faucet

Toilet

Clothes washer

Tub/shower

Sink faucet

Wall

To outside spigot

All taps off main line are ½-in. pipe.

Main line, ½" pipe

To water heater

This is the design you don't want, with ½-in. pipe for the main line. If you find this cold-side setup during your renovation, replace the main lines with ¾-in. pipe.

The ¾-in. pipe on the left provides approximately twice the water flow of the smaller ½-in. pipe. A larger pipe also lowers water velocity, noise, and pipe wear.

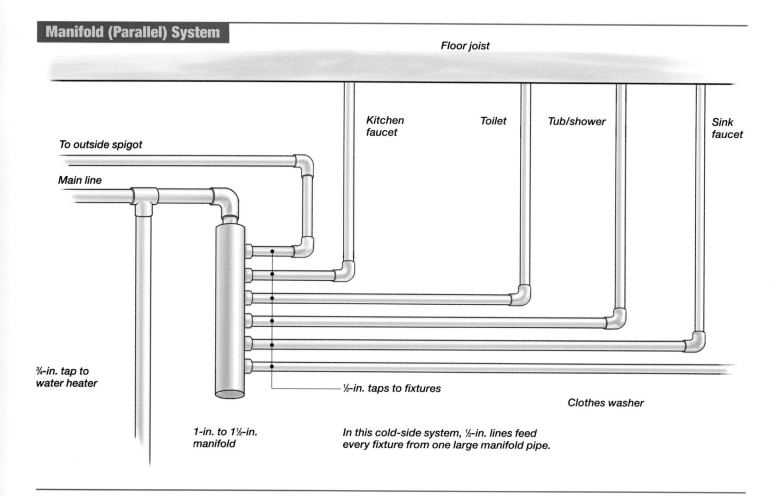

Manifold (Parallel) System

Floor joist

Kitchen faucet

Toilet

Tub/shower

Sink faucet

To outside spigot

Main line

¾-in. tap to water heater

½-in. taps to fixtures

Clothes washer

1-in. to 1½-in. manifold

In this cold-side system, ½-in. lines feed every fixture from one large manifold pipe.

up with occasional loss of pressure and a few hot/cold spurts when water is used in more than one location at the same time.

The design of a basic series system is simple. It uses ¾-in. pipe from the point where water enters the house and for the main run throughout. Because the pipe feeds more than one fixture, its diameter should be ¾-in. Then ½-in. pipe is used to feed only singular fixtures, with the exception of undercounter taps, such as a dishwasher feeding off the kitchen faucet line.

In a poorly designed series system, you will typically see ½-in. pipe everywhere—even for the main line runs. It is this mistake that gives series installations a bad name, as my new customer found out. If during a renovation you inherit this type of installation, you will need to replace all ½-in. main water lines with ¾-in. pipe.

Only the taps to the fixtures should remain ½-in. pipe.

One of the biggest drawbacks of the series system is its problem with velocity. With all the house water flowing through a single pipe, the velocity tends to get too high, which creates noise and erodes metal fittings, especially those made of copper and brass.

The Parallel System

The parallel distribution system uses a costly manifold, made up of a short large-diameter (1-in. to 1½-in.) pipe with many small-diameter pipes branching off from it. From the manifold, individual ½-in. lines feed each fixture in the house. This design works well and solves the water-pressure/volume problem of a poorly designed series system. But with so many ½-in. pipes going everywhere, the

A manifold sends a ½-in. pipe to each fixture in the house.

installation looks like a bowl of spaghetti, and material and labor costs increase. The parallel system generally uses several times the quantity of ½-in. pipe used in the series system. To keep the layout from getting confusing you must mark the destination of each line at the manifold valve so that, for instance, when you turn the valve marked "SINK1" you'll know that you're actually controlling the water to that particular sink and not to the shower.

A well-designed parallel system may require more than one manifold. And now the system gets even more confusing and messy. Typically, there is just one manifold at some central location, distributing both hot and cold water. I prefer to have two manifolds at two different locations: one where the main water line enters the house, just past the shutoff valve for the cold water, and another at the water heater output for all

the hot-water lines that go to the hot side of each fixture. But no matter where you install the manifolds, they must be accessible for maintenance.

Manifolds can be purchased premade or you can make them yourself. I have done both, so I can say the easiest and cheapest alternative is to buy them premade. Though it is expensive, I recommend including a ½-in. ball valve on each ½-in. line that leaves the manifold. Some manifolds have all the ball valves built in, which is the best way to go. If your house has multiple baths, you may need an additional manifold to obtain enough outputs. This brings us back to the main complaints about the manifold system: the complicated installation and the high cost. Basic manifolds cost around $30, whereas the larger, more complicated models retail for around $300.

Customized Installation Rules

▪ Before you run the main water line in the basement or crawlspace, stub out all fixture taps through the floor first. Make them long enough to extend below the floor joist by several inches. This allows you to see all the places you need to tie into.

▪ To make sure the stubouts stay exactly vertical (below and above the floor) and don't fall through the floor, cut some 6-in. blocks from a 4x4 (or three nailed-together 2x4s). Drill a straight ¹¹⁄₁₆-in. hole through the block center. Extend the ½-in. pipe through the holding block and the hole in the floor. If needed, put a couple wraps of tape around the pipe so it can't fall through the block. Extend the pipe a few inches below the joist

so you'll be able to tee into the proposed main water line. These blocks can be premade at home or in a shop and installed as soon as holes are drilled through the floor. After the pipe is glued into the pipe system below the floor, slip the block up and over the pipe for removal.

▪ To determine which stubout is hot and which is cold, wrap a piece of blue tape on the cold pipes and red tape on the hot pipes where it will be visible from under the floor. As you face the faucet, hot is on the left and cold is on the right, but remember it will be the complete opposite if you are looking at the back of the fixture.

Installing Stubouts

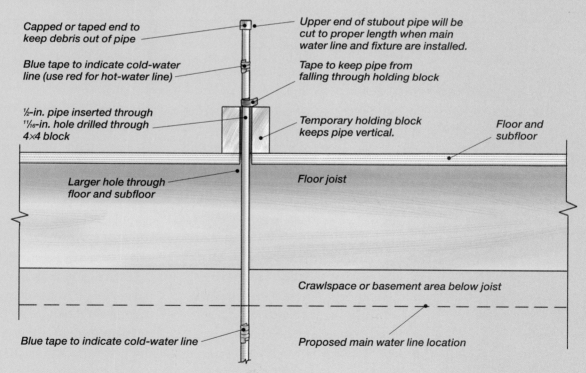

Capped or taped end to keep debris out of pipe

Upper end of stubout pipe will be cut to proper length when main water line and fixture are installed.

Blue tape to indicate cold-water line (use red for hot-water line)

Tape to keep pipe from falling through holding block

½-in. pipe inserted through ¹¹⁄₁₆-in. hole drilled through 4×4 block

Temporary holding block keeps pipe vertical.

Floor and subfloor

Larger hole through floor and subfloor

Floor joist

Crawlspace or basement area below joist

Blue tape to indicate cold-water line

Proposed main water line location

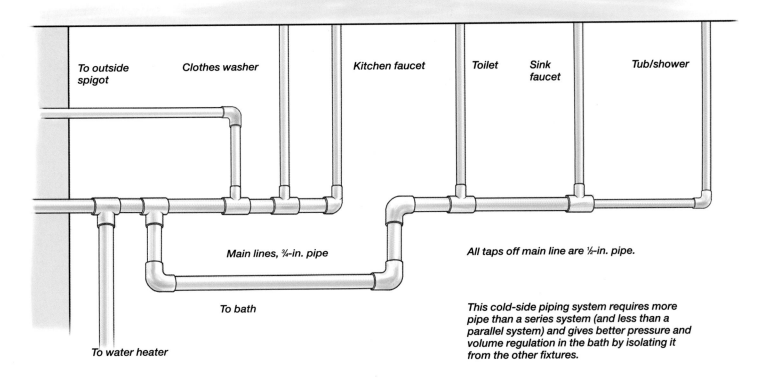

To outside spigot

Clothes washer

Kitchen faucet

Toilet

Sink faucet

Tub/shower

Main lines, ¾-in. pipe

To bath

To water heater

All taps off main line are ½-in. pipe.

This cold-side piping system requires more pipe than a series system (and less than a parallel system) and gives better pressure and volume regulation in the bath by isolating it from the other fixtures.

Customized System

Both the series and parallel systems do their intended job well. But for those of us who value an abundant supply of pressure and volume—so that it's possible to take an extended shower while water is being used elsewhere—and who don't care for the complicated manifold design, a better system is called for. So I developed a system of my own.

START WITH ENOUGH WATER AND SUPPLEMENT, IF NECESSARY Check out the house's water source and make sure there is plenty of water (see "Boosting Your Hot Water Supply" on p. 166). If the water needs of a house sometimes outdraw the small utility water line to the house (for example, a house located at the end of the utility distribution line), you will need to tee

in a large bladder water tank where the utility line enters the building. This tank will help supply the short-duration water needs of the house when demand exceeds what the utility can supply.

In extreme situations, I have installed a 1,000-gal. polyethylene tank (it looks like a miniature submarine) in the basement. Inside this semiclear tank, I placed a submersible pump. Utility or well water slowly fills the tank 24 hours a day, and the submersible pump delivers the water to a bladder tank and to the house. This system handles massive water needs for a significant duration, such as what you may need when all those relatives come for Christmas and Thanksgiving.

INSTALL ENOUGH MAIN WATER LINES Typically I run three main water lines from where the water enters the house (or from the tank outputs as in the example on the facing page). I have one full-size cold line going to the water heater, another full-size cold line going to the bath, and a third going to the kitchen/utility room/half bath. I add a fourth full-size cold line if there is a second full bath upstairs or downstairs.

On the hot-water side, a full-size line goes from the water heater to the kitchen/utility/half bath and to each full bath. With hot-water lines, distance creates problems. Long runs mean a long wait for the water, and a lot of wasted water. So if the kitchen is more than 80 ft. from the water heater, I install a second small water heater in the kitchen, usually under the counter. The drawback with my system is the expense. It cannot be offered on low-bid jobs, only on custom jobs. If the distance from the water heater exceeds 100 ft., codes require an expensive recirculating system for the hot water. In that case, it would be cheaper to install the water heater in the kitchen.

Improving Water Pressure

I hate low water pressure. Low pressure affects everything in the house. The dishwasher and clothes washer take forever to fill. The outside hose squirts an anemic 2 ft., and the shower turns into a small sprinkling device. To increase pressure, first try simple, local solutions at point of use. If those don't work, more drastic measures are called for.

Factors That Reduce Water Pressure

Ever wonder why you have less pressure in the upstairs shower than in the basement? It's because it takes more pressure to get the water all the way up there. For

Water pressure can be lost as the pipes rise to the upper floors of a house.

By the time the water reaches the second-floor showerhead, the pressure has gone down an additional 4 lb.

29 lb.

By the time the water gets to the first-floor showerhead, the water pressure has gone down about 7 lb.

33 lb.

40 lb. of water pressure coming into the basement at around floor level

40 lb.

every 2.31 ft. of vertical climb in your water line, you lose a pound of water pressure. Thus water that enters the house at the basement level loses 11 lb. to 12 lb. by the time it travels to a second-floor showerhead. If your house water pressure is already at the low end—40 lb. would be low and 80 lb. would be high—this is a significant loss.

Now let's add in a water softener and an iron filter. These water-conditioning units each decrease water pressure by about 5 lb. of pressure; therefore, we lose another 10 lb. of pressure after water conditioning.

If the water pressure entering the house is sufficient (50 lb. to 80 lb.), you could survive the pressure loss. But in rural areas where incoming water pressure might dip down to 30 lb., there will be a problem. If added to this there are other poor conditions, such as too small or clogged pipes, improper valves, or poor showerheads, the flow may be reduced to a trickle.

Pinpointing the Problem

To determine whether or not the city water supply to the house is responsible for the low-pressure problem, cut a T into the main water line right after the main shut-off valve. Into the center of the T, install a water-pressure gauge. The gauge will give you a reading of any pressure drop in the system right where the water comes into the house. For example, if the gauge shows a dip in water pressure for a few minutes after you flush the toilet, then you'll know the problem is with the water coming to the house. If the gauge shows no such drop, then the problem must be with the house lines. They may be too small in diameter or fittings, such as globe valves and stop and waste valves, may need to be replaced with full-flow ball valves. Or if you have galvanized pipe, there is a good chance that rust deposits inside the pipes are decreasing the inside diameter of the pipe and restricting the water flow.

Local Problems

Sometimes a pressure problem can be solved locally. For example, low pressure at one faucet is often the result of a clogged screen at the tip of the spout. Clean it or replace the aerator. In the shower, the most common problem is a water-saver showerhead. This device conserves water by forcing the flow inside the showerhead through a tiny hole; the restriction kills all the pressure. Though this device has its place in the city, it can make a rural low-pressure problem intolerable. A restricter can be unscrewed from the head or drilled out.

Another common showerhead problem is an obstruction, such as sand and iron particles that get stuck in the head itself, that reduces the flow to a trickle. If you have hard water, which contains lots of minerals, you will have occasional problems with mineral buildup around the holes in the showerhead. Soak the showerhead in vinegar for a couple of hours to dissolve the minerals. Or simply replace the showerhead; some good-quality models sell for less than $10. The best ones sell for around $35 and up.

In a low-pressure water system, water restricters within fixtures can reduce both pressure and water volume to unacceptable levels.

Whole-House Problems

If the low-pressure problem affects all the fixtures in the house, then it is not a local point-of-use problem. It is either low pressure at the point where water enters the house or something is restricting the water in the main line. If the pipe feeding the house or serving as the main line within the house is old galvanized pipe, then the problem is likely an accumulation of iron deposits within the pipes themselves. The deposits can be so thick that the water is just barely getting through. The solution is to replace the pipe. If the pressure problem affects a group of fixtures in one area, the culprit is probably the branch feeder that supplies those fixtures. To solve this problem, you will have to find the one affected pipe and replace it—and perhaps all the pipes it feeds. If the corroded pipes are within a wall, the most common solution is to cut the pipes off flush with the wall and plumb in a new pipe through the floor to the fixture. See "Cutting through Walls or Floors" on p. 25 for tips.

If the pipe that enters the house is ¾ in. or larger in diameter and if it is made from polyvinyl chloride (PVC), copper, or polyethylene, then it is unlikely the entry pipe is the culprit because these pipes do not fill up with iron deposits. However, I have seen instances of low water pressure/volume caused by polyethylene splitting, PVC cracking, and copper corroding through. The most common place for polyethylene to split is within 3 ft. of the house where dirt tends to settle, pulling the pipe down with it. Buried fittings, such as an underground coupling or elbow, are also high on the leak list for any pipe.

Rural Problems

Rural areas tend to have more water-pressure problems than urban centers. For one thing, rural systems often rely on pumps, whereas city folk have utility companies. If your house has a jet pump, then you may have to live with the problem. You'll know you have a jet pump if you can see and hear the pump. The other type of pump, a submersible pump, is installed down in the well; you can neither see nor hear it. The only way to improve the water pressure in a house on a pump system is to adjust the pressure switch.

Houses at the End of the City Water Line

Though low-pressure problems are more common in rural water systems, city water systems are not immune. Urban houses that sit at the far end of the city

Rural-style water-pressure tanks can be installed on city water systems to add extra water for short duration high-demand periods.

■ **WORK SAFE**
■ **WORK SMART**

The best place to check for unobstructed water pressure is at the tub. There are no restricters or screens in the tub spout.

Adjusting a Pressure Switch

Rural water systems use a pump to push water into a water-pressure tank (pressurized with air). The pump turns on at a low pressure of around 30 lb. and off at around 50 lb. Thus the pressure you feel in the house and at the shower will fluctuate. The pressure is adjustable at the pressure switch, which is located adjacent to the pressure tank. To raise the system pressure, first turn off the power to the pump and remove the cap on top of the pressure switch. Here you will see two threaded posts, one tall and one short, with a nut around each. Do not touch the short post. To increase water pressure, give the plastic nut on the tall post a clockwise turn. Each complete turn will increase water pressure by about 2 lb. When done, put the cap back on the pressure switch.

If you raise the pressure of the water, you must also raise the air pressure in the tank if you have a bladder tank. The rule of thumb here is that you need 2 lb. less than your cut-in pressure (the pressure indicated on the tank's pressure gauge when the pump turns on). Thus if you raise the cut-in pressure of the pressure switch to 40 lb., you want 38 lb. of air in the tank. You must check the air in a bladder tank only after the power to the pump has been removed and the system has bled down to 0 lb. of water pressure (the air is trapped above the bladder and does not bleed out with the water). If you have an old-style galvanized tank, you don't have to do this. You will notice, however, that the tank will attempt to waterlog faster, and you will have to shoot in air on a more regular basis to compensate.

Once done, turn the power back on. If the tank takes more than 5 minutes to fill, return the system to the way you found it. Either the well can't give you enough water or the pump is worn out and can't get the pressure up.

You can increase the size of the water storage tank, but that will not necessarily raise the pressure. It will give you more storage water, which will minimize pressure fluctuations and will be helpful if the power goes out.

To increase water pressure on a country pump system, you must adjust the pressure switch.

water line or tap are often affected. To add a boost for handling temporary water-volume problems, I install a water-pressure tank to store extra water—similar to those used in the country. The tank won't actually increase the pressure, but the extra water will help boost the volume which, in turn, helps keep the existing pressure up. Install the tank right after the main shutoff valve.

Booster Pump

To actively increase the water pressure, you will have to install a booster pump. Installing a booster pump on a city water system, or even a rural water system that uses gravity-fed water, is quite easy. All you do is take the main water line as it enters the house (after the main turnoff valve) and feed it into a jet pump or booster pump. The output of the pump goes to a water-pressure tank, and the output of the tank then goes to the house water pipes. The disadvantage of such a system, if you are used to the constant pressure of city water, is that you now have *fluctuating* water pressure. But the lowest pressure will still be higher than what you had before, and the upper end may be 20 lb. higher. Typically, a booster system can increase your pressure by 50 lb. to 70 lb., if needed. Expect to pay around $800 or more, plus labor. For fitting-by-fitting instructions, see "Installing a Booster Pump," on p. 164.

This booster pump (common jet pump) is taking 30 lb. of incoming street pressure and raising it to 75 lb. for the house.

Water-conditioning systems significantly lower the house water pressure.

■ WORK SAFE
■ WORK SMART

Install the ball valve in such a position that the lever can freely rotate to turn the valve off. Do not install it where the handle will jam on something as it turns 90°.

ACCORDING TO CODE

The main shutoff valve and the valve at the water heater need to be full-flow valves.

■ WORK SAFE
■ WORK SMART

To keep water pressure at its maximum, install only ball valves throughout the water system.

The Problem with Water-Conditioning Systems

Water-conditioning systems are a major contributor to water-pressure loss. Of course, manufacturers rarely advertise this juicy bit of information. As I noted earlier, you'll lose a minimum of 5 lb. of pressure as water flows through all the unit's pipes and tanks. With a multi-conditioning system you can lose up to 10 lb. When I install a conditioning system in the country (pump system), I always try to raise the pressure at the house's point of entry by 10 lb. If your house is supplied by city water, you will have to either live with the problem or install a booster pump.

The Valve Factor

I once did a service call for which the complaint was low water pressure. The system was brand new—the customer had put it in himself. Wanting to be able to isolate every line in the house, he must have had 20 valves cut in. His logic was good; it's nice to be able to isolate a water problem using valves. But the wrong type of valve means lower pressure and less water volume. He used globe and stop/waste valves, which slow or restrict water pressure. I replaced every valve in his system with a ball valve, and the problem was solved (see "Ball Valves Are Best," opposite).

Water Noise and Water Hammer

Few things are more annoying than water noise and water hammer. I have been in some houses where vibrating water lines sounded like a herd of stampeding buffalo. Metal lines are the worst.

The Origin of the Problem

Noisy water is water that is moving too fast for its own good. Water velocity increases when water lines and fittings are too small, and the sound is magnified when the water rushes through the 180° turns within globe and stop/waste valves as well as elbow fittings within the water lines. When the problem is really bad, your house sounds like the background soundtrack of a horror movie.

Around 50 years ago, ½-in. pipe was adequate for most homes because there were few fixtures and appliances that used water. With low demand on the home's water source, water moved slowly through the pipes. But in recent years, upgrades to pipe diameter have not kept pace with the growing number of fixtures and appliances. The result: an increase in water velocity and an increase in noise.

Ball Valves Are Best

Whenever possible, use ball valves. A ball valve is a full-flow valve, meaning that when it is open water moves straight through the valve without impediments or having to turn corners. The hole through the valve body is nearly as large as the diameter of the pipe, which makes for faster, quieter water flow. In addition, the ball valve's handle is easy to use. Rather than having to turn it four or five revolutions, you simply give it a quarter turn to start the water flowing or to shut if off. When the handle is in a straight line with the pipe and valve body, water flows; when the handle is at a 90° angle, the water is off.

Not all ball valves are created equal. At one time, a major manufacturer was making them so cheaply that the female threaded ends would split open as a threaded pipe was screwed in. I use only thick-walled, heavy-duty Apollo ball valves or the equivalent. They are more expensive, but are worth it. *Warning*: Some Apollo ball valves are made in China. Reports from the field indicate these may be inferior to American-made ones.

Apollo ball valves are the best valves to use in water lines.

Another type of full-flow valve is called a gate valve. This valve has a gate that lifts up or down to turn water on or off. Unfortunately, gate valves sometimes cannot completely shut off the water when mounted in a horizontal position, because debris that has accumulated in the bottom of the valve gets in the way. In some cases, water corrodes the gate valve's threaded shaft so that the shaft breaks off, leaving the valve either permanently open or permanently closed.

Globe valves have a stem that rises and falls to open and close. There is a washer at the bottom of the stem, which fits into the valve seat to shut off water flow. However, this washer may wear out or corrode and need to be replaced.

A stop/waste valve is sometimes used to control water leading to an outside hose bib. As winter approaches, you shut off the valve and open the little waste valve to purge the line of water; otherwise, frozen water can crack the pipe. These valves are available only as globe valves. A modern freeze-proof hose bib eliminates the need for a stop/waste valve.

Most stop valves (also called fixture shutoff valves) are cheaply made globe valves that sometimes break down. Spend a little more for ball-type, quarter-turn stop valves, which will last longer.

Globe and stop/waste valves have internal obstructions that limit water flow, make water noise, and reduce water pressure.

A gate valve has a gate, operated by a threaded shaft (not shown). As the handle is turned clockwise, the large gate extends down and closes off the water flow.

For a quieter water flow, instead of using an elbow fitting (*left*), use a street 45 glued into a 45 to create a long-sweep turn (*middle*). Even better, try two 45s separated by a short length of pipe (*right*).

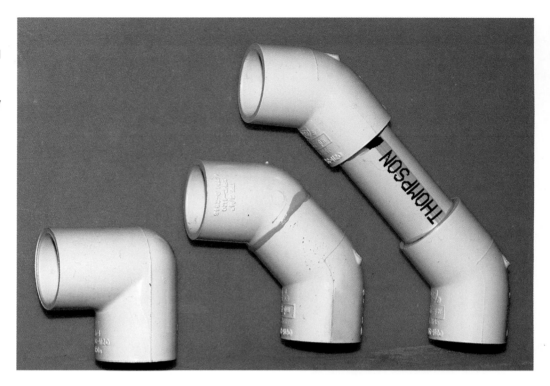

WHAT CAN GO WRONG

If you snug-fit the pipes through the joists and studs, you will hear a squeaking sound for years as the pipes expand, contract, and move within the walls.

Some Solutions

To remedy a noise problem in a straight pipe run, the pipe diameter needs to be increased. Unfortunately, once we increase pipe diameter beyond ¾-in., the cost per foot of pipe skyrockets. For example, 1-in. pipe is more than double the price of ¾-in. pipe.

Another way to decrease the velocity and noise is to install a second ¾-in. main line. As I mentioned earlier, I normally install two ¾-in. main lines, and sometimes I even add a third to handle a extra full bath.

To reduce the water noise through 90° elbows, you can glue (sweat or crimp) a street 45 into a 45, making a long-sweep elbow. Or use two 45s separated by a short piece of pipe.

Vibrating or Squeaking Pipes

Lowering the water velocity—by increasing the number of main feeders, using full-flow valves, and using 45s instead of 90s—solves the water-rushing noise

problem. But it may not stop the pipe vibration or squeaking problem. Vibration is caused by pipes that are not tightly secured. To secure pipes that run under or against joists, see "Strapping Pipes to Joists," on p. 23. When pipes run through holes in joists or studs, the holes have to be larger than the pipes to allow the pipes to expand and contract.

After running pipes through the holes, there are several ways to ensure against noisy vibration. The old-fashioned solution is to make sure the pipe touches nothing or to tap in a shim between the pipe and the hole. The latter will keep the pipe from vibrating, while allowing the pipe to breathe a bit. You can also insert plastic bushings that are made for the purpose. Or squirt insulating foam all around the pipe. This foam adheres strongly yet remains flexible.

A squeaking noise results when a pipe runs through a too-small hole in a stud or joist and rubs against the opening as it expands or contracts. The plumber who installed the pipe may have been too lazy to use the right size drill bit and just used whatever was lying around, or he may have drilled the hole crooked so that the pipe had to be forced through the hole with a hammer. To correct the problem, you may have to remove the pipe from the joist and re-drill a larger hole. Once I had to re-drill an entire house in which 1 year earlier (when the house was built) the lead carpenter had insisted that the plumber keep hole diameter to a minimum to reduce possible structural integrity problems.

Water Hammer

Water hammer makes a sound akin to someone hitting the pipes with a hammer. This problem occurs where there is a fast-closing valve such as a single-handle faucet or washer solenoid. When the valve opens, water very quickly flows to the fixture or appliance.

When the valve closes, the fast-moving water has no place to go, so it smashes into the pipes, with the resulting hammer noise. This problem is common with galvanized and copper pipes, but it also exists in plastic pipe. The noise is not noticeable with plastic pipes; but over time the pipes can suffer damage, so the problem should be addressed.

To correct the situation, install water hammer arresters to add air cushioning. The arresters use air as shock absorbers. By placing them on the hot- and cold-water lines at the fixture or appliance giving the problem (normally where the horizontal stubout pipe—the short horizontal pipe that leads to the fixture shut-off valve—exits the wall), the water now has a place to go—against the air cushion of the arrester. These are recommended even if you have plastic pipe.

Years ago, small vertical air-filled pipes were used as water hammer

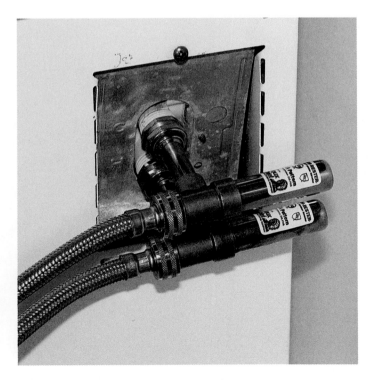
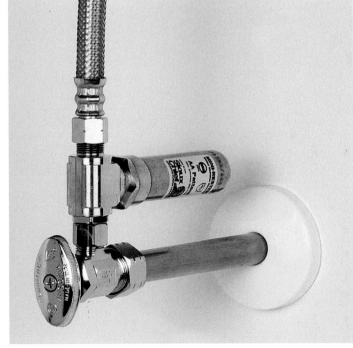

A water hammer arrester can be installed immediately behind the clothes washer. Install one on both the hot (not shown) and the cold valves.

Distribution Line Basics

When running the main lines under the floor joists, sometimes the line can be run directly under each stubout. Another option is to run the line between the stubouts and then run taps horizontally to each.

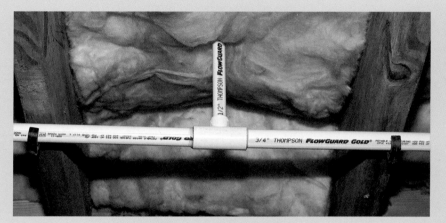

This is the ideal situation. Run the main line right under the stubout for the fixture and tee straight up and in.

If you can't access the main line under the fixture stubout, get close and tee off sideways and then elbow up to the fixture.

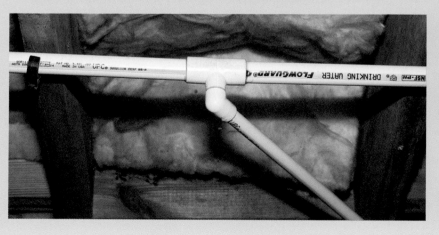

If you can't tap into the main line opposite the stubout, insert the T where you can and run the fixture line at an angle to get to the stubout (not shown).

arresters, but they were useless. The little air they trapped was absorbed into the water in a matter of weeks. Only in the past few years has a system been developed that is capable of keeping the compressible air cushion isolated from the water. These new arresters come with copper sweat, male and female threads, compression, chlorinated polyvinyl chloride (CPVC) glue-on, and hose bib connections, which can connect directly to the pipes right behind the clothes washer or anywhere else on the line. Under a sink, you can often install an arrester on the stubout. I do not suggest installing arresters inside walls since the connections may leak and require maintenance.

Water hammer can also occur within a faucet body. This happens with old-fashioned faucets when a "button" comes loose. The button is the circular disk washer that seals off the water flow inside the faucet body as the handle is cranked down. The button is held tight on the handle assembly bottom via a small screw through its center. If this screw becomes loose, the washer will vibrate as water flows—creating a water hammer noise. Simply remove the collar of the faucet (water is first turned off at the stop valve or water main), then unscrew the handle, and the washer will be seen on its bottom. Tighten its attachment screw back down.

WORK SAFE

Do not use an auger bit if you are using a pistol-grip drill—it's too dangerous—use only spade bits. If you need to use an auger bit, use a right-angle drill to power it.

Drill ¾-in. holes for ½-in. pipe and 1-in. holes for ¾-in. plastic, copper, or PEX pipe. Always drill the holes parallel to the stud, joist, or beam edge to keep the holes in the center of the board.

Stop Valves

Stop valves, also called fixture shutoff valves, are typically installed under a sink or toilet, where they control one hot or cold line leading to the faucet or toilet. They come in either angle (90°) or straight configurations. Pipe coming out of a wall will typically require an angle stop; if the pipe comes out of the floor, you'll want a straight valve.

Stops come in almost any attachment configuration: sweat or compression (for copper pipe), female threaded (for galvanized pipe), crimp (for cross-linked polyethylene; PEX), and glue-on (for plastic pipe). Sadly, most stop valves are of poor quality. I have lost count of the number of stops that were so corroded the handle would not turn. Many

times I have broken off the handle with a pipe wrench trying to open a stuck valve. (To turn a stuck handle, loosen the collar under the handle, turn the handle, and retighten the collar.) Another problem with low-quality stops is that they tend to leak after you leave—as if they had a mind of their own. If left alone they do just fine. But once the handle is turned, pieces of mineral buildup break off internally and water starts to seep out of the stop, commonly around the stem.

High-quality stops come in under $5, so there is no excuse for using the low-quality ones. A ball-type, quarter-turn stop valve is recommended.

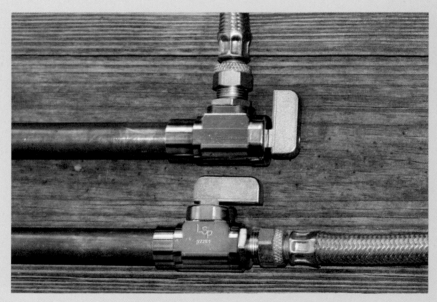

Use heavy-duty, solid-brass quarter-turn ball valves instead of common stop valves.

There are many different types of stops, and all come in two configurations: straight and right angle. Shown here are (left to right) plastic, glue on, barb, female thread, compression, and sweat.

Strapping Pipe to Joists

There are many methods of strapping and securing pipe, depending on whether you want the pipe to be insulated with snap-around insulation or hidden in the house insulation or secured directly to the joist or hanging from it. Don't make the mistake of securing the pipe directly against the joists if you are going to add insulation later.

By far, the fastest method of securing water-pressure pipe directly against a joist is via tube talons—little plastic snap-around clamps with an integral nail. I first tack them in place along the proposed pipe route. Later, when I know they won't move again, I drive in the nail. U-shaped plastic and copper clamps are also available but require nails for installation, which slows you down.

Some manufacturers make plastic J-hooks that snap onto the pipe and enable the pipe to hang from joists. Copper U-hooks are also available but are hard to install properly. They have to be hammered into the joist, and they keep bending to the side. Based on experience, I would recommend using tube talons for securing pipes directly to wood, and common low-cost plastic or galvanized strapping when you want to add insulation onto the pipes.

For securing a water line, nothing is faster than a tube talon. It snaps around the pipe and comes with an integral nail for easy attaching.

Above: **Use plastic or metal strapping for low-cost support when running water lines that need room for insulation.** *Below:* **Once all lines are installed, simply lift the pipe from its strapping and slide on the foam insulation.**

ACCORDING TO CODE

If the water line is less than 1¼ in. from the edge of a stud, it must have a ¹⁄₁₆-in.-thick steel plate to protect it from nails and screws.

Insulating Water Pipes

If budget permits, all water lines should be insulated. Insulation helps keep cold water cold and hot water hot, and it prevents condensation from dripping off pipes and rotting wood. Insulation also improves energy efficiency.

I use only one type of pipe insulation: closed cell, snap-around foam. This product comes in different lengths and simply snaps around the pipe. It can be purchased with or without peel-off tape. If it has no tape, you will need to secure the edges of the insulation with duct tape. Most times you do not have to cut the insulation to go around corners, just bend it. The disadvantage is price, it costs as much if not more than the pipe it is insulating.

Forget using wrap-around fiberglass. As you tightly wrap the pipe, the fiberglass compresses and you lose all the insulating value. In addition, once the fiberglass gets wet, it holds water and becomes a conductor, not an insulator.

If you plan to insulate the pipes, remember that when you install the pipes, they must stand off from the joist or stud. If you attach a pipe directly against a joist or wall, you will not be able to insulate it.

Contrary to popular opinion, insulating pipes will not always prevent them from freezing. It just slows the freezing process. If your pipes have not yet frozen, the temperature simply hasn't gotten cold enough for long enough. And that's the logic of insulating the pipes: You forestall freezing for a period of time until daylight returns or the temperature rises. The only way to completely prevent pipes from freezing over an extended cold spell is to have a heat source.

Closed-cell foam insulation snaps around the pipe for fast and easy installation. However, it costs as much as the pipe itself.

Cutting through Walls or Floors

When running pipes through walls or floors, the first rule to remember is to always drill in the center of a stud or joist—never on the edge. This helps maintain the structural integrity of the wood and keeps nails and screws from damaging the water line. Any hole less than 1¼ in. from the wood edge needs a steel plate for water line protection. For ¾-in. pipe, drill a 1-in. hole. For ½-in. pipe, drill a ¾-in. hole. Be sure that you drill in the exact center of a framing member and that the holes are no larger than 1 in. in diameter in a common 2×4. In a vertical stud or beam, this means drilling one hole on top the other. Do not drill holes side by side in a vertical framing member. Drilling off center or using a bit larger than recommended will position the pipe dangerously close to the stud edge. Do not try to use a smaller bit and squeeze the pipe through a tight hole. As the pipe expands and contracts, it will make a squeaking noise that carries throughout the house.

If possible, avoid drilling basement or attic joists for water lines. The joists probably already have their fair share of holes for wiring. Instead, either attach pipes to them or hang pipes from them. Allow extra room, if needed, for pipe insulation, but never cut a hole large enough for the pipe insulation to go through. A hole that large would compromise the structural integrity of the joist or stud.

Choose the Right Bit

Sharp spade bits are fine for cutting through studs and joists for the water lines. The ones with the two sharp protrusions off each side cut faster than the flat-bladed ones. If you hit a nail, either sharpen the bit or throw it away and get a new one. Spade bits are cheap, and it's not worth the trouble to keep using a dull one. For deeper holes you will need either an auger bit or a spade bit with an extension. Extensions come in 6-in. and 12-in. lengths.

Notch with Great Care

There are times when you will not be drilling, but notching the edge of the stud or joist to keep the pipes forward in the wall. This is dangerous for several reasons:

- It will weaken the wall or joist if you notch too deep; try to limit the notch depth to less than 1 in.
- It puts the pipes in harm's way, vulnerable to protruding nails and screws. For protection, place a steel plate over the pipes for at least the width of the stud.
- Any vibration will go right into the finished wall.
- If the pipes undergo condensation, the sweating water will run directly down the finished wall and rot the wall out.

■ **WORK SAFE**
■ **WORK SMART**

Pipe insulation is sometimes more expensive than the pipe itself. If possible, run the pipes up through the insulated joist cavity and let the house insulation do double-duty—but never in an outside wall in an area that experiences freezing weather.

WHAT CAN GO WRONG

On one job, the insulation contractors stapled the fiberglass batts directly to the plastic water lines. You can imagine what happened when the lines were pressurized.

WHAT CAN GO WRONG

As you turn the handle of a gate valve round and round to turn the water supply off to the house, the threaded shaft inside the valve snaps as the gate inside the valve seats. The valve is in a permanently closed position until it is replaced or fixed.

CHAPTER 2

Tapping into the Supply Lines

BEFORE YOU TAP INTO a water line, you'll need to turn off the water supply to the whole house and drain away the water sitting in the pipes. As my uncle Bud, a veteran remodeler, used to say, "You can't just turn the water off; you have to get rid of it." He would add that getting rid of the water was a three-step process. First, turn off the water at the main. Second, drain off the residual pressure by opening spigots. Third, let gravity drain the water from the lines from the lowest point in the system.

These steps may sound simple and straightforward, but in fact, there are a number of potential problems. In this chapter I will steer you around the many pitfalls I have encountered over the years.

The cutter wheel must make just one single track around the pipe.

Turning Off the Main

To turn off water to the whole house, you must find the main shutoff valve (also called the cutoff valve, or just "the main"). Look for it close to where the water line enters the house. The shutoff valve should be a full-flow valve—either a gate valve or a ball valve. When you turn the handle on the main, be careful not to turn it too far. If the cutoff valve is a gate valve, you will feel the gate seat as you turn it off (turning clockwise); do not turn the handle beyond that point or its internal shaft (from handle to gate) may snap. If the shutoff valve is a ball valve, turn the handle 90° to the pipe.

Draining the Lines

Once the water has been turned off, the next step is to open *all* the fixture faucets. This releases the residual pressure in each water line branch and helps break any vacuum that might be holding water

Turning Off City Water

Some cities do not want you to turn off the main at the water meter (but I do it anyway); they want to do it themselves. If you arrange for them to do it, be prepared to wait a long while both for the turning off and for the turning back on. To turn the water on or off at the water meter, you may need a special long-handled wrench (available at most hardware stores for about $7). In a pinch, you can use a simple adjustable or basin wrench—it just makes the job a lot harder.

in the lines. If the clothes washer is in the basement, turn the washer's dial to run it, and listen for the sound of the solenoid buzzing as the water enters. Wait a few seconds, then turn the washer off. An outside spigot is also a good place to drain the water.

Even with the faucets open and a drain valve or two open in the basement, some water will remain in the lines where there are U-shaped loops. Have a pan ready to catch the water when you cut into the lines.

ACCORDING TO CODE

The house main valve and the water heater valve must be full-flow valves (either a gate valve or a ball valve).

■ WORK SMART

If you turned the water heater off, put a note on your steering wheel reminding yourself to turn the water heater back on before you leave.

Turning Off Rural Water

In the country, water comes from a pressurized water tank filled via a pump. There should be a main shutoff valve at the pressure tank. If not, you can cut off the pump's power via a breaker or fuse. With luck, the power box is marked. Jet pumps—the ones you can see or hear—are often powered via a cord and plug that can be pulled out from a receptacle. Some are wired right into a common switch. Just trace the cord from the pressure switch (the gray box attached to the pump) to see where it goes. If this is not possible, you may have to call an electrician. If all else fails, you can throw the main power switch.

WHAT CAN GO WRONG

If you don't remove the residual pressure after you turn off the main valve, you will get an unexpected shower when you cut into a line.

Which Pipe to Use

There is no such thing as a perfect water supply pipe. Each manufacturer claims its pipe is best and promotes its benefits. But what they are not telling you is the pipe's disadvantages—and each pipe has these as well. In the chart below, I list the advantages and disadvantages of three common pipe materials and include some comments based on my experience using them. Once you have weighed the pros and cons, you can make your own decision about which pipe to use.

Of course, be sure that your pipe choice conforms with local plumbing code, which can vary widely from locale to locale. In many parts of the country, copper is the only acceptable supply pipe. In other areas, PEX or CPVC is allowed or

Pipe Materials: Advantages and Disadvantages

Material	Advantages	Disadvantages
Copper	Beautiful when installed properly	Can change OD when frozen
	Hard to damage physically	Expensive
	Not damaged by ultraviolet light	Aggressive water eats it
	Soft copper can be snaked through joists and studs without cutting	Hard and labor intensive to install
		Has to be reamed after being cut with tubing cutter
	Long rolls are available for running under a slab	Easy to install wrong
		Is a conductor, thus needs to be electrically grounded
		Being metal, heat is easily lost through pipe wall, unless insulated
CPVC	Less expensive than thick copper	Cracks easily when frozen
	Easy and fast to install	Damaged by ultraviolet light
	Unaffected by aggressive water	Cannot take physical abuse
	A nonconductor	Tends to harden after it has been installed
	Being plastic, heat is not easily lost through pipe wall	Cannot use common pipe dope on its plastic threads
		Long rolls, for runs under a slab, may have to be special ordered
PEX	Less expensive than thick copper	Damaged by ultraviolet light
	Will take a moderate to hard freeze without breaking	Cannot take physical abuse
	Installs extremely fast	Easy to install improperly
	Unaffected by aggressive water (but the metal fittings might be)	Must buy special, expensive tools for installation
	A nonconductor	Tools are proprietary—each manufacturer has its own
	Extremely flexible, can be snaked around	
	Being plastic, heat is not easily lost through pipe wall	
	Long rolls are available for running under a slab	

even recommended. If possible, find out the pipe that your local inspector likes best and go with that.

Working with Copper

There are three different types, or grades, of copper pipe—graded according to thickness. Grade K (green lettering on the pipe) is the thickest, followed by Grade L (blue lettering), and Grade M (red lettering), the thinnest. Grade K is too expensive for common residential use. L and M are the common choices. All low-bid project uses Grade M pipe. There would be no need for different thicknesses were it not for the fact that, over time, copper dissolves into the water, and this thins the pipe.

Choosing Soft Copper or Rigid Copper

Copper comes in rolls (called soft copper) or in sticks (called hard or rigid copper). Soft copper is often referred to as "tubing," and hard copper is generally

called "pipe." Both work just fine, but due to the higher cost of soft copper (and its tendency to kink as you unroll it), you will normally work with hard copper within the house.

The exception is when you have a long run under a concrete slab, extending from one side of the house to the other. Then, you would use rolled copper to minimize the number of joints under the slab. Joints are always potential leak spots, and under a slap they are obviously difficult to access. Protect the copper from the corroding effects of lime in the concrete by encasing it in some type of sleeve wherever it is in contact with the slab. I normally use foam pipe insulation. This sleeve also protects the pipe from kinking.

Bending Soft Copper without Kinking

Try not to make significant bends in soft copper using your hands; the pipe will normally kink. Instead, use a spring-type bending tool that slips over the pipe or an electrician's conduit bender. If the

WHAT CAN GO WRONG

If you don't get all the water out of a copper water line, you may not be able to solder it. The water cools the pipe, so it cannot reach the melting temperature of the solder.

Insert the soft copper pipe through a hollow spring and gently put pressure on the spring to bend the pipe.

An electrician's conduit bender can be used to bend Grade L rigid copper.

A mechanical handle, which pulls a supply pipe around a circular hub, makes a perfect bend.

pipe kinks anyway, discard the kinked section; do not try to reuse it.

To bend a section of small-diameter pipe, such as you would use for supply tubes, use a small mechanical hand bender.

Bending Rigid Copper

To make a turn with stick copper, you can sweat on a 90° or 45° elbow for each turn. Or you can use the same electrician's conduit bender I mentioned above. The thinner the copper, the easier it is to bend; you might not be able to bend K or L pipe. If you have room, make two 45° bends instead of a single 90° turn. This makes bending easier and keeps the stretching and compressing of the pipe's metal to a minimum.

Expanded and Damaged Copper

If a copper pipe has kinked, cut out and replace the damaged area. If the pipe has a minor problem—for example, if it has become oval or has expanded slightly from freezing—a flaring tool may be able to restore the end of the pipe to its original shape. To correct the problem, insert the affected pipe end into a flaring tool and tighten down. The tool will squeeze a small section of pipe back to the right size. Slide the tool farther down the pipe and repeat the process. By the second repetition, you should have enough pipe squeezed back to its original size to insert the fitting fully on the pipe. If not, repeat the procedure.

Whether frozen and expanded or bent into an egg shape, the end of a copper pipe sometimes can be brought back into shape with a flaring tool.

Fittings for Copper

There are innumerable types and sizes of fittings available, but basically all fittings are designed to do just a few tasks—join sections of pipe together, change direction, and achieve a transition between different sizes or different materials. Both roll and stick copper can use either soldered (sweated) fittings or compression fittings.

Rolled copper, but not stick copper, can also use flare fittings. These are often used for gas lines but can also be used for water lines. Flare fittings require special tools and are best left to the pros. It's best not to use the cheap flare tool you see in hardware stores. Instead, use a professional tool (which can be obtained from a professional tool supplier) that has a breakover tension design, which allows the handle to freewheel the second you obtain the perfect flare. In my experience, it is best to insert the pipe ½ in. to ⅟₁₆ in. beyond the tool just before you clamp it down. This compensates for the loss of pipe length as the sides flare out to 45°. In addition, always use the heavy-duty flare fittings instead of the cheap ones. Heavy-duty fittings cost $3 to $5 each and require heavy-duty nuts as well (about $1 each). Cheap fittings are half the cost and come with thin, easily split collars.

In most cases, a soldered joint is preferable to a compression joint. Code generally requires that compression joints be accessible, not buried in a wall or floor. However, if there is water in the line or if it is difficult to protect nearby flammable material, sweating (soldering) can be difficult or dangerous. In these cases, you may be better off using compression fittings. Also, if a faucet is located less than 2 ft. above the connection, heat from soldering could travel up and damage the faucet's seals; in that case, opt for a compression fitting or wrap a wet rag around the pipe to act as a heat sink.

Creating a Leak-Free Sweat Joint

Sweating copper is a skill that you can learn in less than an hour. It is not difficult, but it requires methodical attention to detail. To create a leak-free joint, most of the work must be done before the torch is lit. Follow these three rules: cut clean, ream clean, and sand clean.

The three rules of preparing a pipe for sweating: cut clean, ream clean, and sand clean.

The long handle of a common tubing cutter prevents it from being used on installed copper pipe in many locations.

Even a mini-tubing cutter cannot cut pipe adjacent to a wall.

CUTTING By far the best way to cut copper pipe is with a cutoff or chopsaw with a solid metal-cutting blade. (A hacksaw is not recommended; it tends to make jagged, less-than-straight cuts.) This method is fast, clean, and straight and doesn't create a ridge on the inside of the pipe that needs to be reamed out. If the pipe is already installed or if your work must be done in a tight location, use a tubing cutter. The common tubing cutter will need 6 in. to 8 in. of clearance to swing its handle around the pipe (the longer the handle, the easier it is to make the cut). If the location is too tight to accommodate a tubing cutter, you will have to resort to a smaller tubing cutter or even a mini-reciprocating saw.

Common Cutting Errors

Cutting errors happen often, even among pros. There are two common errors to avoid when using a tubing cutter: First, jamming the pipe against the back of the cutter, instead of centering it between its two rollers; and second, overtightening the knob, which jams the cutter wheel against the pipe. The tool must be snug only. Once snug, make two to three circles around the pipe (to start the cut into the pipe body) and verify that the cutter wheel is making a single track. If there are multiple tracks, the pipe cutter is faulty. Repeat until the pipe is cut. If the cutter wheel is dull, replace it.

To ensure a proper cut, the pipe must be between the two front rollers (*arrow*), not jammed against the back of the cutter as seen here.

Open the tubing cutter wide enough so you can slip it over the pipe. Align the cutter's wheel with your cut line, and tighten the tool until the cutter wheel just starts to bite into the copper. Slowly turn the tubing cutter a complete revolution around the pipe, taking care that you turn straight; each time around, the cutter wheel must cut into the same groove. Tighten a slight amount again, turn again, and so on until the pipe breaks off.

REAMING A tubing cutter does not make a perfect cut. It leaves a significant rounded bead along the inside of the pipe that needs to be reamed off. I rarely use the fold-out reamer that may be attached to the tubing cutter because it generally won't cut away all the raised lip and tends to jamb and cut gaps. The best way to ream a ½-in. or ¾-in. copper pipe is with a stepped drill bit powered by a cordless drill. It's fast and easy. You can also use a circular rat-tail file—and I have

Cutting in Tight Spaces

A mini-tubing cutter has no handle, so it can spin around the pipe in tight locations. But with only a thumbwheel to tighten the cutter blade onto the pipe, it is quite difficult to use. I normally have to resort to pliers to turn the handle. The mini-cutter comes in two basic sizes: the first is designed to cut pipe up to ½ in. The second cuts both ½-in. and ¾-in. pipe. Since both tools are the same physical size, it's best to buy the latter tool because you will be working with both sizes of pipe.

Even the mini-cutter needs at least 1 in. of clearance around the pipe to swing its body. To cut a copper pipe in the tightest locations, I use a mini-reciprocating saw made by Makita. Its tiny blade allows me to cut the pipe even when it is tight against a wall. Plus its thin blade and tiny teeth prevent the pipe from jerking as the blade cuts. On the negative side, the blades are brittle and break easily.

If you can get the blade of a mini-reciprocating saw behind the pipe (you need about ¼ in. of space), you will be able to make the cut.

Cutaway view showing a significant ridge on the inside of the pipe left by a tubing cutter.

A stepped drill bit is the perfect tool for reaming out the ridge left inside copper pipe that was cut with a tubing cutter. The bit works for both ½-in. and ¾-in. pipe.

Paper-Thin Copper Pipe

I have done many jobs for which the copper pipe was so thin (eaten away by the water), it couldn't be cut with a tubing cutter. Thin pipe caves in at the slightest pressure. Pipe in this condition has been eaten away by active water for so long that it either has developed pinholes or is about to get pinholes. This most commonly occurs immediately above a water heater. If this is your problem, all the copper should be replaced. If you want to try to cut thin copper, use a very fine toothed metal-cutting blade; even then, you may not be able to connect any fittings to the pipe.

Open-mesh waterproof plumber's cloth works best for cleaning the outside of a pipe.

All copper fittings, even new ones, need to be cleaned inside the socket with a specially designed wire brush.

The Best Cleaning Products

Mesh Plumber's Cloth

There are several varieties of plumber's cloth. The mesh cloth cleans better than the solid cloth and allows the grit to fall away. Avoid the non-waterproof option; this cloth dissolves as it gets wet and contaminates the pipe.

Circular Wire Brush

Plumber's cloth doesn't work for the inside of a fitting because your finger is too big. Use a circular wire brush, available to fit both ½-in. and ¾-in. fittings. Insert the brush all the way into the fitting hub and turn at least six full rotations. Replace the brush if the end becomes rounded or dirty.

WHAT CAN GO WRONG

A wire brush or plumber's cloth that is dirty or worn out will not get the fitting clean enough and may even contaminate it. As a result, the solder will not flow right, and the joint may leak. Keep these supplies in a clean bag when not in use.

done so on many occasions—but it is labor intensive.

CLEANING Once the pipe has been reamed and its edges smoothed, it's time to clean the parts of the pipe and fitting that will receive solder—the interior of the fitting and its lip, and the exterior of the pipe. *Clean* in plumbing jargon means brushed heavily with a plumber's wire brush and/or waterproof sanding cloth (called plumber's cloth). Once the fitting or pipe is clean, be careful not to set it on something dirty or to touch the cleaned surface with your oily, sweaty, dirty fingers. This is probably the most common error committed by do-it-your-selfers, and even some pros.

Do not make the mistake of assuming the fitting is clean because it is new. This is a common, major amateur mistake. Though it is shiny, it is not what plumbers call clean. It still must be wire brushed or sanded. The same "clean"

This fitting is not clean! Though new and shiny, it has unseen surface oxides that will inhibit the solder flow.

logic is used for your hands. Just because they are not obviously dirty does not mean they are clean enough to touch a cleaned fitting or pipe edge. Your hands have oil on them that will be transferred to the cleaned copper and inhibit a properly sweated joint.

■ WORK SAFE
■ WORK SMART

Here's a bad habit to avoid: Peeling or breaking off a large section of solder and wrapping it around your hand. This wastes solder and recontaminates cleaned solder.

Buying Solder and Flux

Buying the right solder and flux can put the odds in your favor for obtaining a high-quality sweated joint. Look for solder with a low melting temperature and a wide working temperature range (the temperature range within which the solder can flow once it melts).

The most common solder, 95/5, melts at around 450ºF. I use a product called Oatey Safe Flo which has a lower melting temperature of 415ºF. This means I don't have to heat the joint as hot for the solder to melt. The 95/5 product also has a narrow working range: around 16º.

Oatey Safe Flo has a working range of around 40º. This broad temperature range provides more tolerance for getting a good joint.

For flux, I use an Oatey product called No. 95 Tinning Flux. This flux doesn't burn off like common flux (common flux will vaporize and burn black on the pipe if heated too hot) and has silver particles within to tin the pipe, allowing the solder to flow faster and easier and to cover all the contact area. When I solder, I like to have all the odds on my side.

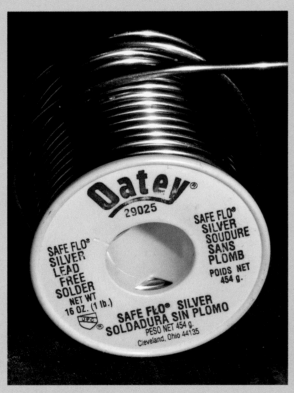

Put the odds on your side by using a solder with a low melting point and wide working temperature range.

Reduce the job stress by using a flux that won't burn and a joint with silver, which allows the solder to flow faster and better.

Sweating Techniques

Sweating is an art form, and a properly sweated joint is a work of art. You can read about sweating/soldering all you want, but the only way to get good at it is to practice, practice, practice.

After a pipe has been cut straight, properly cleaned, and reamed, it is ready to sweat. To melt solder, you don't need a fancy bottle of special gas that heats to 1,000°F or more. Solder melts at around 450°F, and a common propane bottle with a push-button torch head (or common torch head with striker) will do the trick. To be safe, use low-temperature, wide range solder (see "Buying Solder and Flux," opposite).

GETTING SET TO SWEAT Keep in mind that heat transfers. Thus other fittings near the fitting you are sweating will also heat up. This is to your advantage if you are soldering a T-fitting or both ends of a coupling or elbow. If you are attaching to a fitting that already has one of its joints sweated, protect that joint (heat can also "un-sweat" a joint) by wrapping it with a wet cloth, and keep it wet. Do the same for any other nearby fittings. You will know the instant such a joint becomes unsoldered because the old dull-looking solder will become a shiny silver color. Normally, if you allow the joint to cool naturally and do not jar the pipe, it will resolidify without creating a leak. In

Working Safely with High Heat

■ Before you sweat a joint, be sure there is nothing behind the fitting that can be burned. For protection, use a fiberglass antiburn cloth (made just for the purpose), a piece of tin, or a piece of concrete block.

■ Antiburn cloths and tin stop fire but not heat. If high heat will damage what is behind the joint being sweated, use a 1-in.-thick concrete block for protection.

■ A common error that even the pros make is installing pipe tight against a wall. Doing so means you have to burn the wall, joist, stud, or whatever, to solder (or resolder) the joint. Plus you will not be able to put insulation around the pipe.

■ Accidents can happen. I once caught an entire wall on fire and, another time, a field of grass. Always have a fire extinguisher nearby when you sweat a fitting.

■ When you sweat a fitting, be sure that children and flammables are out of harm's way.

■ Never assume the flame is out just because you can't see it; valves sometimes leak. That's how I caught the field afire.

The two best ways to protect against flame: a fiberglass cloth and a concrete block.

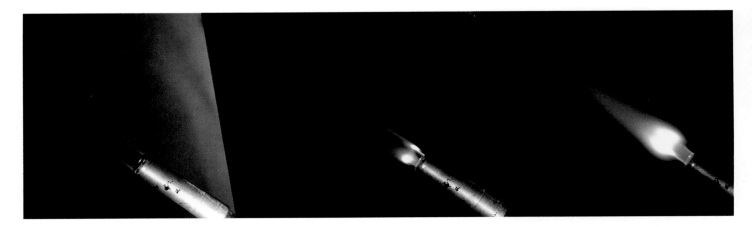

Left: **When the flame arcs up, caused by not enough pressure, open the valve more.** *Right*: **When the flame has too much pressure, close the valve a bit.** *Middle*: **This is a workable flame.**

■ WORK SAFE
■ **WORK** SMART

Torch heads are fragile. Wrap them in a dish towel and store them in a lidded plastic container.

■ WORK SAFE
■ **WORK** SMART

If working over a finished floor, place something underneath the joint you are sweating to catch any solder drips.

worse-case conditions, you may have to reheat the old joint and add a small amount of new solder.

Although capillary action (the ability of a fluid to flow against gravity) will pull solder in any direction, including up, it is always best to work with gravity on your side. If possible, the hub end should point up or, if that's not possible, the pipe and fitting should be in a horizontal position. If neither is possible, you'll have to sweat the pipe/fitting in a vertical position with the hub pointing down and hope that capillary action will pull the solder up into the joint (and it normally does).

The different colors of the flame, from yellow to blue, indicate different temperatures within the flame. The distant yellow tip is a lower temperature. The hot blue tip is what needs to make contact with the fitting. You can control the heat applied to the fitting by adjusting the blue flame. The more blue, the greater the heat transfer. Many newer-model torch heads have been adjusted so that blue is all you will see. Adjust the flame by adjusting the pressure (simply turn the knob on the handle). When you light the torch, observe the flame and listen to the noise. If the pressure is too low, the blue flame will arc up at its tip and the noise will be minimal. If the

pressure is too high, the flame will broaden out at the base and be very noisy. You want something in the middle: as sharp a point as you can get on the blue flame, with moderate noise. The length of flame will depend on the torch head— from 2 in. to 4 in. is common.

SWEATING STEP BY STEP

1. After cleaning the fitting and pipe as described earlier, apply flux to the surfaces to be joined, using a small clean brush. Join the pipe and fitting, then twist the fitting to spread the flux evenly and orient the fitting correctly. Remove excess flux with a clean rag.

2. Turn on the torch and adjust the flame. Preheat the pipe for a few seconds (heat it first because it is the largest mass), using a back-and-forth motion to apply the blue part of the flame to the pipe. Then apply heat to the fitting hub for a few seconds, sweeping the flame back and forth along the surface.

3. Back off the flame and drag the solder over the joint to see if it melts. If it doesn't, reapply the flame for a few seconds more to both the pipe and the fitting.

Eventually, the parts will be up to temperature (around 450°F) and the solder will melt and flow. If you cannot get the junction hot enough to melt the solder, there is probably water in the lines, which is absorbing the heat.

4. When the solder starts to flow, remove the flame. You want the solder to flow but not get too hot. You will use ½ in. to ¾ in. of solder. If the solder starts to pool and drip from the bottom of the fitting or run down the pipe, remove the solder; you're done sweating.

5. Wipe the fitting and the pipe with a *dry* cloth. A wet cloth can cool the fitting too quickly, possibly causing a leak in the solder. Once the fitting is back to room temperature, remove any excess flux with a rag dipped in some undiluted oil-cutting dish-washing detergent, such as Dawn.

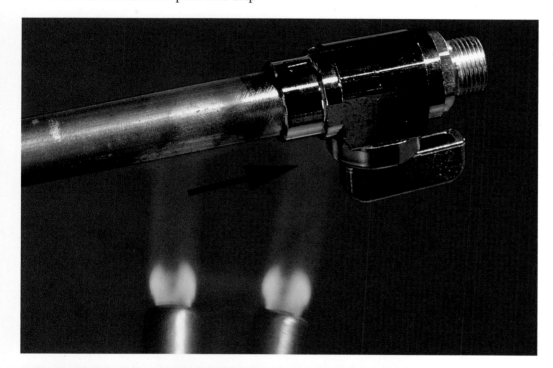

Heat the pipe first (left flame) and then move torch head to just above the joint (right flame).

Stop adding solder the moment you see a drip start to form.

A Leaking Sweated Joint

If a sweated joint leaks (water sprays or drips out of the connection), you must completely drain the system and start over. If you can't get all the water out, you must cut the pipe, drain the water, and resweat the joint. If there is just a very small amount of water in the pipe, I have been able to heat the pipe to boil the water and steam it out.

After a couple of unsuccessful soldering attempts, you may have ruined the pipe and fitting for sweating purposes (it will be discolored and blackened from overheating). If you are completely unable to sweat it properly, either cut the fitting and pipe away and start over or consider using a compression fitting instead of a sweat fitting.

If the fitting is burned and overheated, yet still leaks, you will have to cut the fitting away (along with some of the pipe) and resweat.

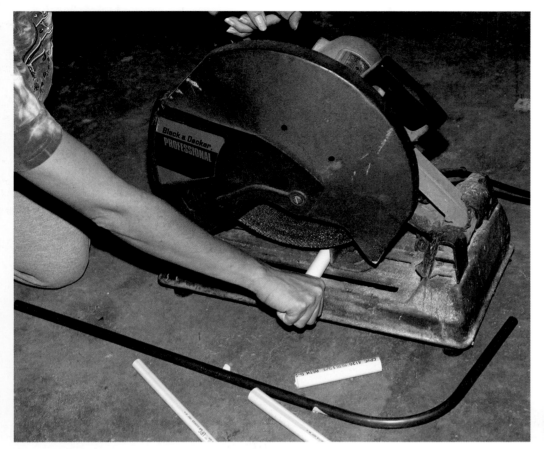

A solid-blade cutoff saw is the best pipe cutter for CPVC and copper.

Working with CPVC

CPVC (chlorinated polyvinyl chloride) is normally what we are talking about when we mention plastic pipe. It has been around since about 1960, when the first polymer was patented by BF Goodrich. Since then, CPVC has been manufactured under license by various companies. It is used for both hot- and cold-water piping, including the hot-water relief valve pipe in water heaters.

CPVC comes in both rolls and 10-ft. sticks. Sticks, being straight, make for a neater installation. Rolls work best for long runs under a slab (rolls may have to be special ordered). Do not make a CPVC connection under a concrete slab. As the CPVC angles up from beneath a slab or wall, sleeve the pipe with ½-in. foam insulation so the concrete does not touch it.

Store pipe away from sunlight and areas where it might take physical abuse. CPVC will shatter or crack when hit under very cold conditions. For example, do not put this pipe on an overhead rack and let it bounce around as you drive to the job site in the wintertime.

Cutting CPVC

By far the best tool to use for cutting CPVC pipe is a chopsaw or cutoff saw. The cut will always be straight and clean. A miter box works well, also. Unfortunately, both tools work only for pipe that is not yet installed.

If the pipe is already in place, then you must use ratcheting scissors. These make a clean cut, especially compared to a toothed cutter like a saw, but they have two big disadvantages. First, even with a razor-sharp blade, they have a hard time cutting a small piece off the edge of a

■ WORK SAFE
■ WORK SMART

Keep all CPVC fittings in large, sealable plastic containers. This keeps the fittings clean and in one spot. I like to use three plastic bins: one for ½-in. fittings, another for ¾-in. fittings, and a third for reducer fittings.

■ WORK SAFE
■ WORK SMART

When you buy pipe, verify it does not have debris inside; then buy and install caps immediately. This keeps out trash and insects until the pipe is put in service. (Mud-dabber wasps love to build nests inside pipe.)

■ WORK SAFE
■ WORK SMART

Be sure to wear safety glasses when using a reciprocating or cutoff saw to cut metal pipe.

Even sharp ratcheting scissors have a hard time cutting a small piece off of a CPVC pipe end.

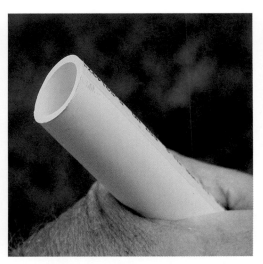

Ratcheting scissors do not always make a straight cut.

A PVC handsaw cuts CPVC just fine, but its coarse teeth leaves a mess at the cut edge.

pipe. Second, it is sometimes hard to make a straight cut across the pipe; the cut normally comes off angled.

There is a trick to using ratcheting scissors. As you apply pressure, use your palm and push the handle down (clockwise) as you cut and pull the pipe up (counterclockwise). For old and brittle pipe, you may need to score a deep ring all the way around the pipe before you cut, to prevent the pipe from ovaling or snapping.

In a pinch, you can use a fine-tooth hacksaw, large reciprocating saw, or mini-reciprocating saw. But toothed blades leave a jagged edge that has to be smoothed and cleaned (see "Cleaning," on p. 37). Do the cleaning work with an open-mesh plumber's cloth. Clean both the inside and the outside edge. Try not to let the tiny plastic slivers fall inside the pipe.

Gluing CPVC

You must use the proper glue for CPVC pipe and fittings. There are two options: Orange-colored CPVC glue requires a coat of primer before the glue can be applied. Flowguard Gold glue, gold in color, does not require a primer. Do not use a multipurpose glue, PVC glue, acrylonitrile butadiene styrene (ABS) glue, or any other glue. Apply glue gingerly, following the instructions below.

When you apply primer or glue to a pipe or fitting, the dauber will at first contain too much liquid as it comes out of the can. Press the dauber against the can interior to try to squeeze out the majority of the liquid. Then apply it lightly, like a thin coat of paint, to the surface of the pipe and fitting. Do not press the dauber hard against the plastic; that might cause the primer or glue to run or pool. If it pools, it will soften the plastic and create a weak joint. Just lightly swipe it around the fitting or pipe, giving it a last swipe for cleanup, to absorb any excess primer or glue.

> **WORK SAFE**
> **WORK SMART**
>
> Both primer and glue are highly flammable and are hazardous to the lungs. Be sure your work area is well ventilated and that there are no flames nearby, and take care not to breathe the fumes.

The orange CPVC glue (*right*) requires a primer. The gold CPVC glue (*left*) does not.

Pull the dauber up against the side of the can's lip to remove excess glue before you apply it to the pipe.

Apply glue to the fitting interior and the pipe exterior. Go around twice and use the third time around to absorb any excess.

Push the fitting onto pipe about 90° off from its final location, then twist the fitting to the alignment mark. Hold the fitting on the for about a minute.

GLUING STEP BY STEP

1. Check that the cut edge is straight and free of burrs.
2. Be sure the pipe has been properly cleaned and that no debris has been left inside the pipe.
3. Dry-fit the fitting onto the pipe and point it in the exact direction it has to face. Mark both fitting and pipe with a slash or arrow.
4. Apply the glue to the pipe, then the socket. Make a couple of circles to ensure that all the plastic has been covered; then make one last circle to absorb any excess glue back into the dauber.
5. Insert the fitting onto pipe a quarter to half turn out of phase from its final position. Once on, twist the fitting to its final position. This helps spread out the glue. Hold the fitting on the pipe for about a minute. If you let go too soon, the fitting may back off the pipe.

Some people don't like the appearance of plastic pipe. To minimize the eyesore effect, you can paint the exposed section of pipe or perhaps keep the pipe in the wall and stub out with finished metal pipe—even copper if you want.

Avoid fittings with all-plastic threads, whether male or female. They cannot handle stress and are prone to crack or split when tightened. Instead use brass male and female CPVC fittings. These have a plastic end into which you can glue CPVC and have brass male and female threads. Brass union CPVC fittings are also available. If you have no choice but to use a plastic male or female fitting,

WHAT CAN GO WRONG

If you drop the dauber into the dirt, do not use it again until you clean it. Otherwise, the dirt and debris will weaken the joint.

Male, female, and compression brass CPVC interface fittings in both ½ in. and ¾ in. sizes.

These brass male adapter-to-compression fittings will allow an interface to CPVC, PEX, or copper.

WHAT CAN GO WRONG

If purple primer spills onto a linoleum floor, the purple will almost instantly etch itself into the floor and cannot be removed. It will also stain carpet, but a clear primer may lighten the purple if applied immediately.

WHAT CAN GO WRONG

Sometimes a fitting is attached to the pipe facing the wrong direction. Solution: Cut the pipe back 6 in. or so, insert a coupling (use a compression coupling, if desired), and turn the fitting the right direction.

Without a pipe inserted into the hub of this plastic male adapter, it will crack easily when tightened into a fitting.

insert a small piece of pipe into the hub end before you tighten it so the hub will not oval out and crack. Even when it is installed without cracking, you will still have to deal with the high probability of the fitting leaking, either now or sometime in the future.

There are two types of glue-on valves for CPVC pipe: the round-handle globe valve and the lever-handle ball valve. Both have problems. The round-handle valve reduces water flow and pressure and is against code in most situations. The lever-handle is a full-flow valve but is difficult to fully turn on and off because the handle sticks (it is possible to insert plumber's grease onto the ball of the valve to make it turn easy). The best method is to interface with high-quality

metal ball valves, but it is a lot more expensive.

Most codes won't allow plastic pipe or fittings within 12 in. to 18 in. of a water heater connection. Instead, use ¾-in. stainless-steel braided pipe (which costs about $10). Galvanized pipe (available at most large plumbing supply houses for about $3) is a cheaper alternative, but braided pipe is superior because both ends of the pipe act as a union, so it's easy to install a new heater when the time comes, and since it is flexible, it is preferred in areas prone to earthquake. Avoid thin copper corrugated pipe; it is commonly sold for this situation, but in active water, it will disintegrate (see "Working with Copper," on p. 29).

Working Safely with Glue and Primer

▪ If you drip glue or primer on a finished floor, you may or may not ruin it. To be safe, always work on top of a large piece of cardboard or the equivalent.

▪ Keep glue and primer in a plastic container in case it gets knocked over.

▪ Provide plenty of ventilation and avoid open flames when using highly flammable glue or primer.

▪ Avoid applying massive amounts of glue on the pipe socket and joint. Excess glue will soften the socket and can gouge out the upper surface of the pipe as the pipe enters the socket. The gouge can then become an obstruction in the pipe that blocks water flow.

Flexible water heater connections. The copper one is extremely thin. The braided stainless-steel connector is preferred.

Always verify that the seals are still in the pipe.

Working with PEX

PEX (cross-linked polyethylene) is per-haps the easiest pipe to work with—bar none. It installs at least twice as fast as any other pipe. But there is one caveat. You have to choose one manufacturer and stick with it for all materials, includ-ing proprietary tools and fittings. PEX parts and fittings are not interchangeable from one manufacturer to the next. However, all PEX, regardless of manufac-turer, has the same outside diameter as copper and CPVC, so a variety of com-pression fittings will interface different types of pipe.

PEX pipe comes in flexible 10-ft. sticks or in rolls of various lengths (depending on the manufacturer). Use the sticks as often as possible because they are much easier to work with. Use the rolls for longer runs to minimize splices. Fittings come in metal or plastic crimp and metal or plastic compression.

The most common connection method where I live is a crimp system

The PEX pipe and fittings for each job must be from the same manufacturer.

that is identical to the old polybutylene (PB) systems. You can distinguish the two systems by the color of the crimp rings. PEX rings are black, and PB rings are copper colored. You can even use the same crimpers as you would with PB. But be sure you do not interchange the fittings. No matter which proprietary system you use, practice connecting a few fittings before you do the real thing.

Installing PEX

Installing crimp-type PEX is simplicity itself; however, you will need to buy a fairly expensive crimping tool. Just cut the pipe to length, slide a ring over the pipe, push the barbed fitting into the pipe, align the ring, and crimp. Most mistakes occur in the crimping. The crimp jaw must completely cover the ring with a ⅛-in. to ¼-in. gap between the fitting

Here's an example of PEX (*right*) to PB (*left*) crimp transition coupling. Note the PEX side has two barbs and the PB side has numerous barbs.

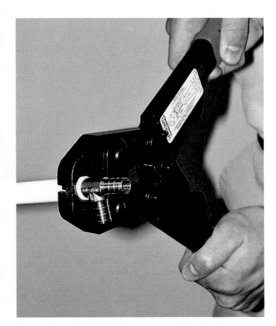

Long-handled crimpers provide the best leverage for crimping.

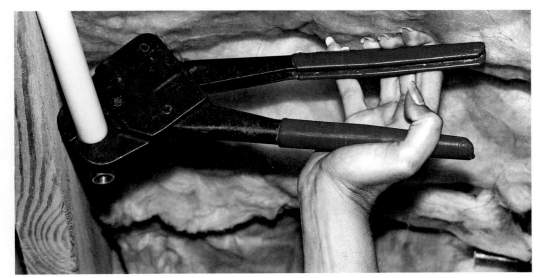

Short-handled crimpers are nice for cramped areas but require an extremely strong hand grip to close.

This is what a good crimp should look like. The pipe is cut straight and has slid all the way on, and the ring is positioned correctly.

WHAT CAN GO WRONG

on't lose the gauge or hex wrench that comes with your new PEX crimpers. The gauge fits over the ring to verify that it is fully crimped. The hex wrench adjusts the crimpers back within tolerance if they squeeze the crimp ring tight enough for the gauge to slide easily over the ring.

body and the crimp ring—no less, no more—so the crimp ring will compress the pipe onto the fitting's two raised rings (or barbs). In addition, the crimpers must maintain a 90° angle to the pipe as the crimp is made.

Keeping the ring from moving while you try to crimp it is often a challenge. What I do is lightly squeeze the ring against the pipe with pliers—just tight enough to keep it from moving out of place. Then I position the crimpers over the ring and crimp it.

Here are a few commonsense rules to use with PEX:

■ Never bend PEX against its natural curve.

■ Always aim for gentle bends.

■ Use plastic supports every 32 in. or closer.

■ Keep the pipe 12 in. away from anything that can get super hot.

■ Never use an open flame on the pipe.

■ Attach a metal protective plate if the pipe is within 1¼ in. of a stud edge.

■ Sleeve the pipe through any type of concrete.

■ Always tee off straight from a fitting. Never tee off at an angle.

Working with Galvanized Pipe

Galvanized pipe is no longer viable for in-house plumbing. It is too expensive and labor-intensive to install and requires very expensive and specialized tools. However, short threaded pieces of galvanized pipe, called nipples, and galvanized fittings, are used in all piping systems from copper to CPVC.

Unless you are going to use a nipple right away, wrap its threads with electrical tape when purchased. This protects the threads from rust and debris and keeps the threads from being nicked and dented. If the nipple comes inside plastic wrap, leave the wrap on until you're

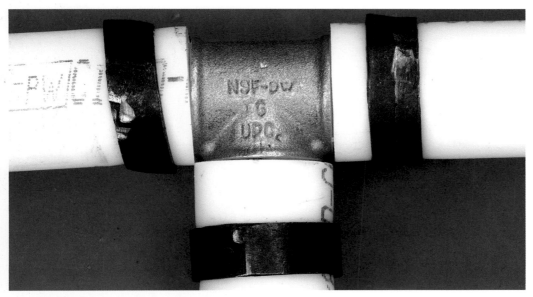

Here are three bad crimps. *Left*: The ring has been crimped at an angle. *Middle*: The ring has been crimped too far from the shoulder of the fitting. *Right*: Only the right side of the ring has been crimped.

ready to use the nipple. Sections of pipe up to 3 ft. long are commonly available at large plumbing supply stores. Many local hardware stores stock and cut galvanized to any length.

If you are removing all the old galvanized pipe in your renovation, use a reciprocating saw with a metal-cutting blade. To speed the process, cut adjacent to the fittings at the pipe threads. This is the thinnest spot on the pipe, and you should be able to cut through in 3 seconds to 4 seconds. I have cut loose all the old piping in a house in under 15 minutes.

It is not a good idea to cut out some sections and leave in other sections because as the reciprocating saw jerks and bangs on the pipe, bits of rust are dislodged throughout the system, and these will clog up everything once the water starts flowing again. If you are trying to tap into an old system, this can be a major problem. It is often best to replace all the galvanized pipe. In addition, old galvanized pipe may be so weak (from rusting out from the inside) that it may cave in as the pipe wrench tries to turn it.

If one section of pipe is that weak, the entire system should be replaced.

If you go against my advice and make a splice into the system, you will need to cut out a section of galvanized pipe between female fittings and splice in a new section of the type of pipe you are installing in the renovation. Then tee into the new section for the renovation or add-on.

A galvanized union-type transition coupling is available that is designed to slip onto cut galvanized pipe. However, I don't recommend using it. I have had several of these friction-fit couplings blow out and off the pipe. This fitting works only if the two pipes sticking into the coupling are fixed in place and cannot move backward. Thus when working with galvanized pipe, always try to tap into or stub off from threaded connections.

Working with Pipe Dope and Tape

The purpose of pipe dope and tape is twofold. First, the lubricant qualities allow the male threads of the pipe to be turned deeper into the fitting to better prevent a leak. Second, the compound keeps the male and female threads from rusting together so that years later, they are not impossible to separate. Common pipe dope comes in a can, and it is spread on the threads with a brush.

Teflon tape provides the same function as common pipe dope but is less messy. Point the threaded pipe end toward you, and wrap the tape clockwise around the threads—that is, the same direction as you will screw on a fitting. I normally go around twice. If it is wrapped counterclockwise, the tape will unwind as the fitting turns clockwise onto the threads. Teflon tape comes in both ½-in. and ¾-in. widths. You will need both sizes—the wider tape is for larger pipe. Some plumbers use both types of dope: first the tape then the paste on top of that.

If you are using pipe dope on gas fittings, verify that it is rated for such. If you use Teflon tape, remember that the common white-colored stuff we use for plumbing is not rated for gas installations. Teflon tape that is rated for gas is normally a different color.

Be wary about applying paste dope to plastic threads unless it is approved for such. Common paste pipe dope will crack the fitting within a few weeks of installation.

Canned pipe dope and tape both work well and are required on any type of threaded pipe or male fitting.

Teflon tape must be installed clockwise on the threads. Otherwise the tape will bunch up and come loose as a fitting is screwed onto the threads in a clockwise direction. Point the threads toward you and wrap downward.

Working with PB

PB (polybutylene) pipe was taken off the market in the United States around 1996. However, many homes still have it, and the product is still installed in Europe. The majority of the problems were with the plastic fittings, but I have also seen leaks with metal fittings. Many plumbers still consider PB as reliable as other types of pipe. I, personally, have installed many thousands of feet of PB with no failure and have also replaced copper, galvanized, and CPVC pipes that weren't yet 1 year old. If the home isn't currently having problems with PB fittings, there is no way to tell whether it will continue that way or leak the next day. If you work with it, try not to bend the pipe, which will stress the fitting/pipe connection, and try not to move the pipe at all. It might cause a leak.

If your house has PB, you will need to decide whether to leave it in place or remove everything. One factor to consider is the condition of the crimp system. If many of the crimped rings are not smooth all the way around the crimp, but instead have a piece of ring squeezed out to the side, the entire system should be replaced. If a great many of the rings are just half crimped— meaning the installer didn't get the crimp tool fully around the ring—the system should be replaced, or at least at those specific connections. If a ring is butted up against the fitting so that it doesn't have the required ⅛-in. to ¼-in. gap, the fitting should be replaced.

Take a look at the T-fittings, too. If the pipe center connection turns sharply to the side, the fitting is under too much stress. The installer should have run the pipe straight from the fitting for a short distance and inserted an elbow, instead of trying to make a tight curve right off the fitting.

If you choose to tee into existing PB rather than replacing it, the connection is not difficult if you use the large gray compression fittings (copper, PEX, and CPVC have the same OD). Simply cut the line, insert a compression T, and come off the center of the T with your new pipe.

Working with PVC

White PVC (polyvinyl chloride) plastic is used primarily for drain and sewer lines and to supply nonpotable water, such as yard sprinkler systems. If rated for water service, PVC can be used to bring water up to the house. However, most codes require that it be terminated within a few feet of where it enters the house to keep it from being used for hot water within the residence.

Always use PVC glue—not a multipurpose glue or other type of glue. Keep your cuts clean and straight (use a solid-blade cutoff saw if possible).

■ WORK SAFE
■ **WORK** SMART

If your area is subject to freezing temperatures, do not run pipe within an exterior wall if you can avoid it.

Though no longer installed new, you will encounter PB pipes and fittings in older houses.

Using Compression Fittings

If the pipe comes into the fitting at an angle, the brass ferrule will be lower on one side than the other, which almost guarantees a leak.

Taking the pipe out at an angle crushed the brass ferrule on one side and not the other, which resulted in a leak around the sleeve.

Because of leak problems with metal ferrules, I believe plastic ferrules are better. Because they are tapered, the small end must always point into the fitting.

As handy as compression fittings are for connecting different types of pipe, they do have a few idiosyncrasies. For example, experience has taught me to stick to an all-plastic body, or at least a metal body with plastic ferrules, because compression fittings with metal sleeves or ferrules tend to leak.

Whether the body of the fitting is plastic or metal, it is absolutely essential that the incoming pipe enter straight into the fitting to minimize leaks. The slightest angle can pull the ferrule over to one side and down, causing uneven compression as you tighten the surrounding nut; this will eventually cause a leak. If you need to turn or bend the pipe, simply leave the first few inches of pipe straight as it goes into the fitting.

In metal compression fittings, leaks are normally caused by the tightening nut being a little too big (due to manufacturer tolerances) for the brass ferrule sleeve. As the nut tightens down onto the fitting body, instead of the ferrule evenly compressing around the pipe to make a good seal, one side of the ferrule slips up on the pipe (and the other slips down), resulting in an uneven seal. This is aggravated further when the pipe is not going straight into the fitting. Metal compression fittings also have a habit of leaking hours or days later. Many times I have had to cut the pipe and discard the end with the squished ferrule and start again. To solve this problem for ⅜-in.-outer-diameter supply tubes, I have changed over to plastic-tapered ferrules, which tend not to leak. If you do the same, be sure to install the tapered end pointing into the fitting.

Another problem with brass compression fittings (by design), either coupling or T, is that often a pipe cannot slide all the way into and through the fitting. The pipe slides into the fitting a short distance and then bottoms out. As a result, if the pipe you are teeing into is locked down and has minimal left and right movement, it is not possible to install a brass compression T or coupling into the line.

I prefer to stick to the large gray compression fittings for ½-in. and ¾-in. pipe. These use a seal and stainless-steel locking ring and a large cone-shaped nut. They are less troublesome than their metal cousins, and they allow you to slide the fitting all the way onto the pipe and then bring it back and center it over the cut. However, since pipe slides in so easily, be careful that you don't accidentally slide a pipe too far so that it cuts off the water supply to one of the lines.

When I first started installing plastic compression fittings many years ago, a few of them leaked. Investigating, I found out what I was doing wrong: The pipe's cut edge has to be perfectly clean and straight. It is imperative that you sand off the rough edges from the copper pipe end before you slide on the fitting's seal. If you do not, there is a high chance the soft seal's undersurface (the surface sliding against the rounded pipe) will be scratched as you slide it onto the pipe. This scratch may result in a leak.

If you made a jagged cut with a hacksaw, then sanding alone is not enough. You also must use a file or small grinding wheel to smooth the edge. It is also a good idea to put a small amount of plumber's grease on the pipe so the seal slides easily along the pipe. In addition, you may want to apply Teflon tape to the threads of the gray plastic fitting to achieve a tighter connection (by breaking the cohesion attraction between the plastic nut and the plastic body). Do not use pipe dope; it can ruin the fitting. *continued . . .*

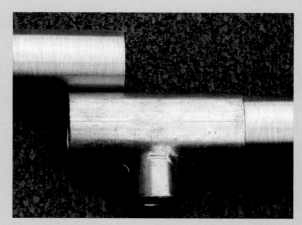

Inserting a T-fitting on a cut copper pipe that is fastened in place is not easy. One end can bend down to slip on the T, but since neither pipe can move left or right, the T cannot slip on the upper pipe.

The type of compression fitting I normally install uses a large angled seal along with a stainless-steel gripper and cone-shaped nut.

Using Compression Fittings *continued*

The large, gray compression fitting slides all the way onto one pipe and then slides back over the cut as the pipes are realigned.

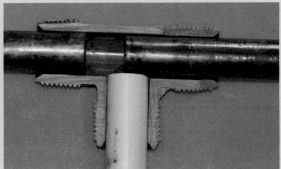

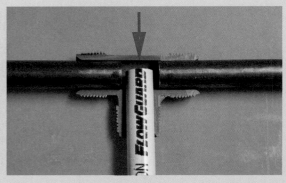

Because the compression fitting can slide fully onto the pipe, it is possible for the pipes to be installed incorrectly in the T fitting. *Left middle*: These pipes are installed at the proper distance into the fitting. *Right middle*: The right pipe is installed too far into the fitting, cutting off some water flow (same problem can occur with left pipe). *Left bottom*: Both pipes are installed too far into the fitting; the center pipe will get no water. *Right bottom*: The center pipe is installed too far into the fitting, cutting off its water flow.

Running Pipes

In a remodel, whether you want to take pipes from one room to the next or from floor to floor, there are many ways to do it. The fastest, easiest, and cheapest way is to leave the pipes exposed. In other words, run the pipes along the trim (the coldest location) or along the ceiling/wall corner (the warmest location), and paint the pipes the color of the wall. However, the aesthetics leave a bit to be desired.

Hiding Pipes

If you want to hide the pipes, you'll have to get a little creative. For just running around the room, oversize baseboard trim can hide pipes quite easily. The baseboard can be finished out with molding.

The big challenge in remodeling is getting pipes up to the second floor from the basement. The best way to hide pipe that runs from a lower to an upper floor is inside a first-floor closet or perhaps through the first-floor utility room. Here

Behind Custom Trim

Pipes can be hidden behind custom trim made from common 1× lumber.

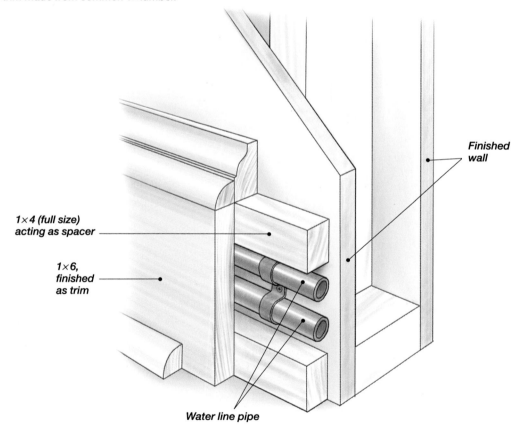

Finished wall

1×4 (full size) acting as spacer

1×6, finished as trim

Water line pipe

In a Corner

Pipes run in a wall corner can be covered with a single board.

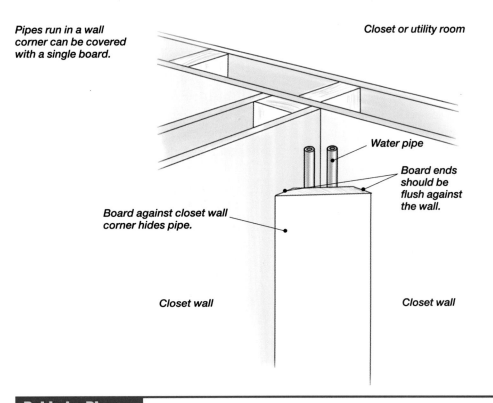

Closet or utility room

Water pipe

Board ends should be flush against the wall.

Board against closet wall corner hides pipe.

Closet wall

Closet wall

Behind a Plenum

On flat-finished walls, you can hide the pipes behind a plenum built from 1× or even 2× lumber.

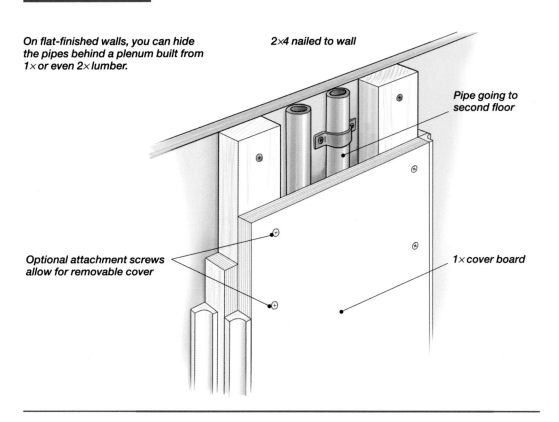

2×4 nailed to wall

Pipe going to second floor

Optional attachment screws allow for removable cover

1× cover board

you can leave the pipes exposed, tuck them in a corner, or hide them under a plenum (a three-sided box built of boards, as shown in the drawing opposite. You will need to decide whether to bring the water line pipes up with the drain line or to run them separately. Either way is fine; the decision probably hinges on where the pipes are in the basement and where they are going upstairs. If the closet or utility room is not in a useful location, you'll have to run a plenum in a living area or go to the trouble of putting the pipes in the wall.

Running Lines through an Existing Wall

Since new plumbing lines are often associated with major remodeling work, you often have access to wall cavities, thanks to the removal of wallboard. But it's still challenging to get pipe up through a stud bay. The first thing I do to make this easier is make a long oval hole in the wall's bottom plate, first drilling a pair of holes and then connecting them with a reciprocating saw, as shown in the drawing below. This larger opening easily accommodates separate hot- and cold-water supply lines.

Create the Wall Opening

A large, horizontal opening is needed in the wall behind the proposed tub to allow enough space to pull the flexible pipe up from the floor below.

Step 1

Drill two 1¼-in. holes in plate.

Step 2

Use a reciprocating saw to make two cuts to open the area between the holes.

Step 3

When complete, the large hole in wall plate will provide easy access for running the pipe.

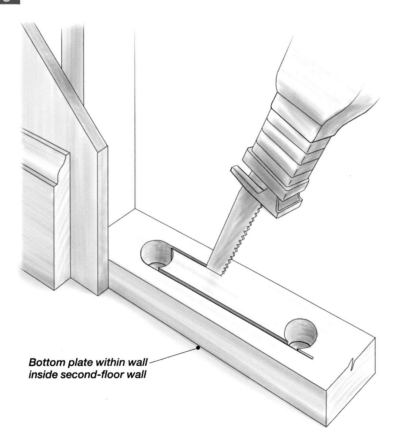

Bottom plate within wall inside second-floor wall

Instead of struggling to install rigid supply pipe in this situation, I use flexible copper or (where code permits) PEX. You can feed the pipe through the opening from above or below. The important thing is to make sure you have enough length to extend all the way through the stud bay (or bays) and to your planned connection fittings.

In rare situations, it's necessary to fish pipe through an insulated wall. You still begin this process by drilling an elongated hole, as described earlier. But

I've found that it's sometimes better to fish your way through insulation with the fiberglass or metal fish tape that electricians use for this purpose. Once the end of your tape makes it through the insulation, you can secure the pipe to the end of the fish tape and pull the line through. Metal fish tape coming off the roll will tend to stay bent. To counter this, cut a long piece of tape off the reel and keep it stored straight. Be sure to cut off the hooked end, which always tends to get itself caught inside the wall.

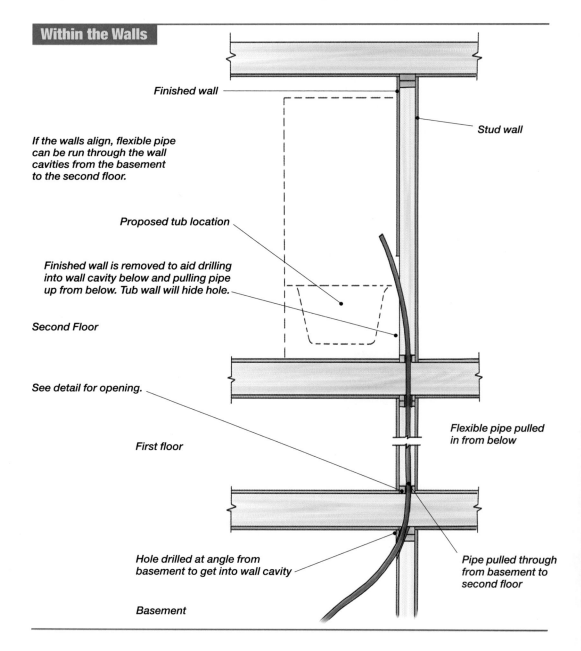

Within the Walls

Finished wall

Stud wall

If the walls align, flexible pipe can be run through the wall cavities from the basement to the second floor.

Proposed tub location

Finished wall is removed to aid drilling into wall cavity below and pulling pipe up from below. Tub wall will hide hole.

Second Floor

See detail for opening.

Flexible pipe pulled in from below

First floor

Hole drilled at angle from basement to get into wall cavity

Pipe pulled through from basement to second floor

Basement

CHAPTER 3

Adding/Running Drain and Vent Lines

N REMODEL PLUMBING you will be cutting into old drain lines to add new fixtures and appliances. Choosing where the actual tap is made is critical. The wrong location can make the job much more complicated than it needs to be and adversely affect the drain system of existing appliances. With three generations of experience to pass along, I will show you how and where to cut into old lines, how to run new lines, and what tools to use. I'll help you identify potential pitfalls and point out helpful shortcuts. Let's start by taking a look at the big picture—and some commonsense rules.

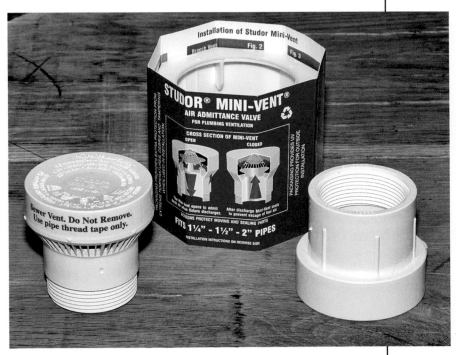

AAVs (1½ in. and 2 in.) can take the place of an individual- and multiple-fixture vent in most cases.

Commonsense Rules

When it comes to drain lines, there is a multitude of little rules, which can be bewildering. Don't worry. You can stay

Working with Inspectors

You may or may not have to get a permit (and pay a fee) to do a renovation. If you are a new contractor or master plumber, the inspector may want to "log you in" to have your numbers on file. If you are new to the game, it's a good idea to prepare detailed drawings of your plans, perhaps including a photo or two. If the situation is unusual in some way, you might ask the inspector to come out and take a look. The inspector will not tell you how to do the job but may tell you what he or she will be looking for in an inspection. Unless you are a master plumber, it rarely pays to argue with the inspector. If you disagree, do it politely and have a solid, logical reason. If you plan to install an air-admittance valve for a vent, be sure to ask first. Even though they work and even though most codes allow them, your specific inspector may not like them, and inspectors have a habit of bending the codes to their likes and dislikes.

Setting the Slope

A spacer on the end of a level allows you to center the bubble to achieve the proper slope for a drain line

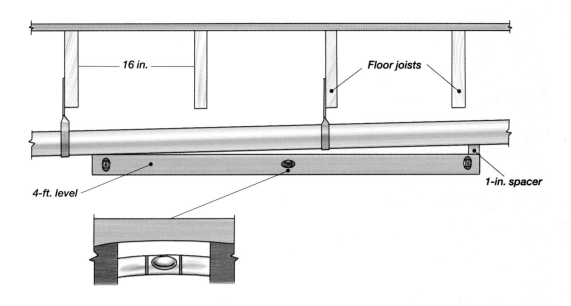

out of trouble and maintain a good design by simply following some commonsense advice.

Install Pipes with a Downhill Slope

The most important rule is to install pipes with a downhill slope; and it should never be violated. Shoot for a *minimum* slope of ¼ in. per foot, which is 1 in. for every 4 ft. Codes may permit a lesser slope—as little as ⅟₁₆ in. per foot—but don't lower your standards. Lines with such a minimal slope have a habit of clogging. A proper slope keeps fluids moving at a "scouring velocity" (calculated by engineers to be 2 ft. per second), which is the speed that helps keep the pipes clean. The scouring velocity also keeps solids in suspension, so they don't

settle. When the velocity is too low, either from inadequate slope (⅟₁₆ in. per foot) or from tremendously oversize pipes (for instance, a 6-in. pipe for a sink), solids tend to drop out of the water and settle to the bottom of the pipe, which can result in stoppages. Once solids have stopped moving, a greater velocity is required to get them moving again. A true scouring velocity should, then, be higher than the velocity initially used to transport solids. The bottom line is: Go out of your way to slope the pipe ¼ in. per foot or more.

For the most part, do not worry about excessive slope. There is no code maximum on slope. Despite what you may have heard, fast-moving water does not leave solids behind. It is slow-moving water (moving slower than 2 ft. per

Level Advice

An Easy Way to Measure for Proper Slope

Attach a 1-in.-thick spacer to the top end of your 4-ft. level and place the level against the bottom of the drain pipe. Center the bubble for a perfect slope of ¼-in. per foot.

An Easy Way to Verify Slope

To verify proper slope and to free up a hand for working, attach a level to the drain pipe using a couple of Velcro straps.

Which Levels Are Good to Have on Hand?

You will need levels of several different lengths: a 6-in. torpedo level, a 2-ft. level, and a 4-ft. level. Keep them within reach. Longer levels are useful for verifying level across floor joists.

Three Common Mistakes

■ Using a level with caked-on debris. If your level (or the pipe you are laying the level on) has debris (such as dried concrete) on its flat surface, you will get an incorrect slope reading. Never use your level to smooth concrete as (I am ashamed to say) I have done.

■ Choosing the wrong place to rest the level. Placing one end of the level on a fitting hub and the opposite end on the pipe will give an incorrect slope reading. Both ends have to be on a hub or on the pipe itself.

■ Trusting your eyes, rather than a level or plumb bob, to reference horizontal or vertical slope. I once plumbed a line downhill by constantly increasing the distance between the pipe and the joists. Visually it looked like the pipe was going downhill. But it wasn't. The floor joists were far off and led me astray. I actually ran the pipe level and in some spots uphill. Shame on me. I never made that mistake again.

second) that causes solids to come out of suspension, not the reverse. High velocity keeps matter in suspension. To quote the IPC (International Plumbing Code): "A drainage pipe can be installed with greater slopes because a maximum slope is not prescribed." The exception to the rule is the horizontal branch line leading from a fixture trap to a vertical vent, such as what you might encounter behind a bathroom or kitchen sink; here you do not want to put the vent intake lower than the trap water (see "Bringing Outside Air into the Pipes" on p. 71).

Be Generous with Pipe Diameter

Keep the pipe diameter as large as is practical and affordable. I normally exceed minimum code by around one pipe diameter. This gives me the added assurance that the fluid within will fill no more than half the pipe, allowing air to freely circulate above the water flow. It is true that excessive pipe diameter will slow water down to the point where the 2 ft. per second rule will be violated and solids may come out of suspension. But this is not a problem in residential housing, for which pipes diameters are kept at 4 in. and under and slopes are kept at a minimum of ¼ in. per foot.

Water Slugs

Air pushed in front of a water slug in a large-diameter pipe also circulates above and behind the slug, so that all parts of the pipe have the same pressure.

Large-Diameter Pipe

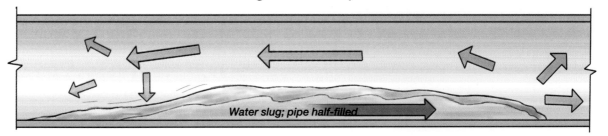

Water slug; pipe half-filled

A too-small pipe filled with water pushes all the air in the pipe in front of the slug, creating positive pressure in front and negative pressure (vacuum) in back.

Small-Diameter Pipe

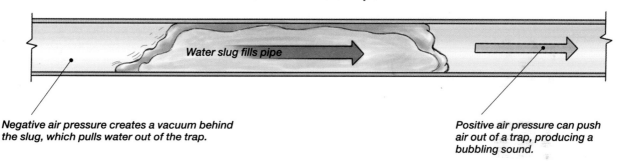

Water slug fills pipe

Negative air pressure creates a vacuum behind the slug, which pulls water out of the trap.

Positive air pressure can push air out of a trap, producing a bubbling sound.

Here's what happens when pipes are too small: As the rushing water (called a slug) flows downstream, it completely fills the pipe, pushing all the air ahead. This pressurized air has to go somewhere. If there is no vent to the outside, it may exit via the toilet bowl, producing the bubbling sound you sometimes hear in a poorly designed system. In addition, as fluids traveling in the pipes push against high air pressure, their velocity is slowed, causing solids to settle and leading to clogs. Behind the slug, just the opposite is happening. The air in the pipe is pulled backward, creating a negative air system, or vacuum, which tends to pull water out of any traps located behind the slug (assuming no vents). When the water in the traps is gone, sewer gas will enter the house. The bottom line is: Large-enough pipe diameters mean no high pressure being pushed ahead, no vacuum being pulled behind, and no problems. In addition, under the IPC, large-diameter drains allow you to use a combination drain and vent system (see "Wet Venting" on p. 81).

Here are some tips for determining pipe diameter:

■ Use either 3-in. or 4-in. pipe to attach to a toilet flange. But as soon as the sewer line goes horizontal, if at all possible, use 4 in.

■ If water from more than one fixture (other than a toilet) will flow through a pipe, the diameter should be 2 in.

■ If you use the combination drain and vent, use no drain lines smaller than 2 in.

■ The minimum pipe diameter in or under a slab should be 2 in.

Unfortunately, when remodeling you will often find that the drain pipe most convenient for tapping into is smaller in diameter than the size pipe you want to install. For instance, you might find an existing 1½-in. pipe where you wanted to tap in a new 2-in. pipe. If there is a larger pipe downstream, you will need to extend your new line to reach the larger-diameter pipe. If this is not an option, you will have to limit the size of the new add-on line to the size of the existing pipe (if possible), or you will have to replace the old run with larger pipe.

COMMON TROUBLE SPOTS The kitchen drain line is normally the longest drain pipe in the house and also carries the hottest water. The heat softens the pipe and makes it sag between supports, especially if the supports are spaced far apart. The low spot will collect food debris, which may eventually close the line. Thus keep the kitchen drain pipe diameter as large as practical, and keep it well supported: every 24 in. to 32 in. when running at an angle to the floor joists and every 36 in. when running parallel to the joists. Code will sometimes allow 1½-in. pipes in the kitchen, but to be safe, these pipes should never be smaller than 2 in. I have lost count of the number of 1½-in. kitchen drain lines I've had to clear or replace with larger lines.

The utility room drain for the clothes washer is another common trouble spot. The washer's drain pipe should never be less than 2 in. in diameter, even though both manufacturer and code may allow smaller-diameter pipe. Keeping it at 2 in. will minimize clogs and will prevent overflow of the high-pressure discharge water from the top of the washer drain pipe. Further, code requires a 2-in. if it is run under the slab.

The line that runs vertically into the clothes washer trap (the vertical standpipe) can also be a trouble spot if it is too short (less than 18 in.). I've never had problems with longer standpipes (42 in. to 48 in. is a typical maximum spec)—

WHAT CAN GO WRONG

The inspector may make you fix a whole lot of stuff (code violations) that already exist in the system. If you are working on a fixed budget or contract price, this could blow your profit or budget right out the window.

Be Aware of Existing Problems

You cannot plumb a good drain system into a bad drain system. Take time to assess the condition of the existing system before you begin your renovation. Take a step back; look at the total situation; and ask yourself, "Is there anything wrong with this picture?" Here are some things to look for:

▪ Pipes that are too small.

▪ PVC that is glued into ABS.

▪ Drain pipes that are improperly supported.

▪ Pipes that might be half-clogged downstream from where you are tapping in.

▪ A system with no main large-diameter vent.

▪ Large drains glued into small drains.

▪ Joists that are drilled or cut in half by a previous plumber.

▪ Improper fittings.

▪ Proper fittings mounted improperly.

▪ Joints left unglued.

▪ Joints that leak.

▪ Sagging kitchen drain pipe.

Think ahead. Once you tap into a drain line, its existing problems become your problems, and you may have to correct them.

only with the short ones. Sometimes the standpipe has to be short; for instance, when the drain line for the washer empties into a high overhead drain pipe. In this case, you'll need to verify that the washer's pump can send the water high enough. Check the washer's specs; normally the capacity is quite high. You might opt for a seal (available at most supply stores) that fits around the washer drain hose where it discharges into the standpipe to prevent any water kickback. If this is going to be inspected, you had best ask the inspector if he or she will pass a short washer standpipe.

Wash the Sewer Lines

My uncle Bud taught me this many, many years ago: "Always wash the sewer lines with the water from another fixture." By this he meant that the line upstream (at a higher spot) from a toilet should always have an appliance or fixture that drains down toward the toilet. Though the typical ¼-in.-per-foot slope will work, a higher slope per foot will increase the velocity of the water and produce a better scour. A clothes washer or tub/shower is ideal, but a sink will also do the trick. The downward flow of water will clean the toilet line, washing away leftover toilet paper or debris so that it cannot accumulate in the line. This home-grown rule is even more important with today's low-flow toilets. In my opinion, this rule is so important it should be inserted into the codes.

Sewer Line Placement

It is always a good idea to wash a sewer line via another upstream fixture. As the water flows downstream, it scours the line and keeps it clean.

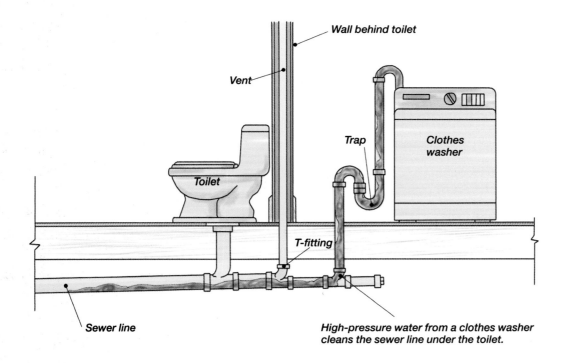

High-pressure water from a clothes washer cleans the sewer line under the toilet.

Intact Trap

To keep trap water intact, use a sanitary T-fitting, do not exceed ¼ in. per foot of slope, and minimize the distance from the trap to the vent .

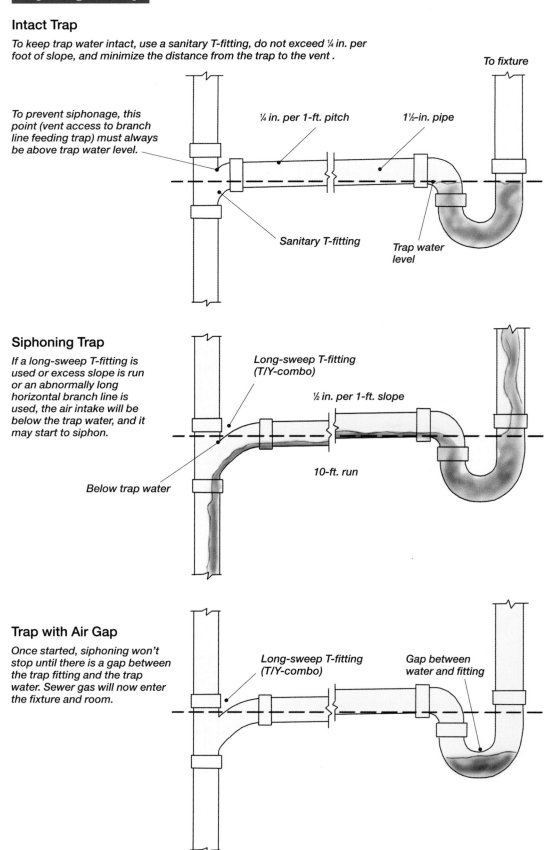

To prevent siphonage, this point (vent access to branch line feeding trap) must always be above trap water level.

To fixture

¼ in. per 1-ft. pitch

1½-in. pipe

Sanitary T-fitting

Trap water level

Siphoning Trap

If a long-sweep T-fitting is used or excess slope is run or an abnormally long horizontal branch line is used, the air intake will be below the trap water, and it may start to siphon.

Long-sweep T-fitting (T/Y-combo)

½ in. per 1-ft. slope

10-ft. run

Below trap water

Trap with Air Gap

Once started, siphoning won't stop until there is a gap between the trap fitting and the trap water. Sewer gas will now enter the fixture and room.

Long-sweep T-fitting (T/Y-combo)

Gap between water and fitting

Bringing Outside Air into the Pipes

To keep all water traps intact—so that air pressure created in the lines when other fixtures are used does not push/pull water out—abundant free air must be available within the drain lines. This is accomplished by venting, or taking pipes from the drain line to the outside air. Each fixture has to be vented to keep the water trap intact.

Here are some basic principles to keep in mind:

- *Distance.* Experience has shown that the distance from trap to vent is critical. If you exceed this distance you run the risk of self-siphonage, meaning the water will follow itself right out of the trap.

- *The right fitting.* It's important to install the right type of fitting where the fixture's water drains from horizontal to vertical (for instance, right behind a bathroom sink where the vent goes vertical).This fitting must be a common sanitary T, not a long-sweep T. The latter will contribute to self-siphonage.

- *Slope.* This is one instance where excessive slope is not wanted because if the T (where the air comes into the line) is made below the trap weir (the water level within the trap), the trap may self-siphon. The maximum distance recommended for all residential drain lines is listed in the chart at right.

Trap to Vent Distances

Pipe/Trap Size	Minimum Distance from Trap to Vent
1½ in. with 1½-in. trap	5 ft.
2 in. with 1½-in. trap	8 ft.
2 in. with 2-in. trap	6 ft.
3 in.	10 ft.

Venting a New Fixture or Plumbing Group

If you are adding a complete plumbing group, you will need one main vent pipe, the same size as the largest pipe in the system. This is normally a 3-in or 4-in. vent that goes through to the roof. Some new codes allow the use of several small vents instead of one large vent; in this case, add up the diameters of the small vents to be sure the sum is equivalent to the diameter of the large vent. My preference is to run one large vent for the system and then to vent each fixture. A main vent pipe typically runs up a wet wall (made with 2×6 studs), which serves as a bathroom wall.

Here are some venting rules to keep in mind:

- An individual fixture needs one small vent, normally 1½ in. in diameter. (Sometimes you can use 1¼ in. for fixtures, but it's normally not worth the trouble of keeping an extra pipe size in stock.)
- The toilet and groups of two or more fixtures require a 2-in. vent.
- Some codes do not want you to run the main vent upstream from the toilet.
- Remember that when you run vent lines the Ts are installed upside down.

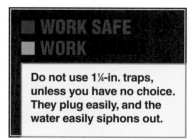

WORK SAFE WORK

Do not use 1¼-in. traps, unless you have no choice. They plug easily, and the water easily siphons out.

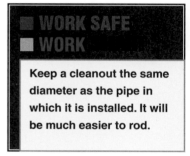

WORK SAFE WORK

Keep a cleanout the same diameter as the pipe in which it is installed. It will be much easier to rod.

Vertical Vent Line

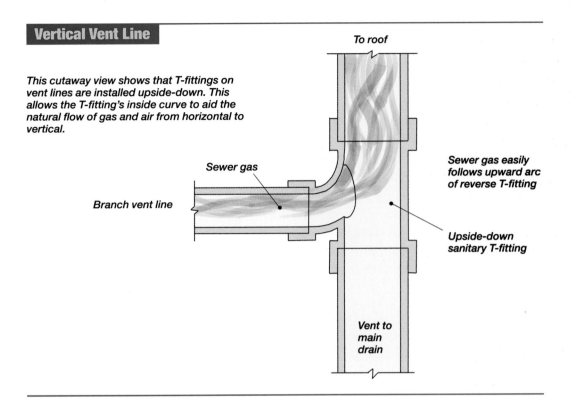

This cutaway view shows that T-fittings on vent lines are installed upside-down. This allows the T-fitting's inside curve to aid the natural flow of gas and air from horizontal to vertical.

To roof

Sewer gas

Branch vent line

Sewer gas easily follows upward arc of reverse T-fitting

Upside-down sanitary T-fitting

Vent to main drain

- Elbows, either short or long sweep, may be used.
- Always pitch the line the same as a drain line.

Hiding the vents in a house that is already built is always a problem. Install the new vent pipe off the top of a T-fitting in the main run, wherever access through the floor is not a problem; for instance, close to a wall. If you're able to install it close to a plumbing fixture, it can also serve as that fixture's individual vent.

When I find I can't fit the large vent pipe inside a wall, I run it up outside the wall in a room corner (from crawlspace to attic) and box it in. The best place for this less aesthetic arrangement is in a closet corner; but if that is not possible, a little creativity can ease the eyesore effect. One customer built a corner bookcase around the pipe. Another painted the pipe to match the wall color. If for whatever

reason you can't get one large pipe through to the roof, you can substitute two 2-in. pipes. If the house already has a large 3-in. or 4-in. vent pipe for the drain system, then the new plumbing group needs only one more 2-in. vent pipe.

You may see a remodel vent line run up the outside siding of a house (in which case the pipe should be at least 2 ft. under the soffit and should not terminate close to an openable window). At one time this was allowed, but not so much anymore. And, of course, it is quite ugly. Typically, this is done to avoid having to climb the roof, which can be quite dangerous.

A lot of vents extending up into the attic and through the roof make your roof look like a pincushion. As an alternative, tie the vents together in the attic, then go through the roof with one large pipe. As a second alternative, you can use air-admittance valves, or AAVs (see "Venting with AAVs" on p. 76). Normally, the kitchen is so far from the bath vent system that it requires its own vent or AAV. Verify AAVs are allowed in your area; although they work very well and are approved by almost all national and international coding authorities, local codes sometimes lag behind or may be extremely conservative in their methods. No matter how many vent roof penetrations you have, it is best to position them away from the main road where they cannot be seen. And if you really want to get fancy, cut the top of the pipe the same pitch of the roof and paint the exposed pipe the same color as the roof.

Sometimes wind will sweep sewer gas from roof vents down to ground level. To prevent this, I have installed a U-bend on the pipe after it leaves the roof, sort of an upside-down trap (a 90 and a street 90), and this seems to work. However, an odor-control filter is now available that fits onto the vent pipe on the roof. I have not installed one and cannot verify that it works.

If it is not possible to run an individual vent, take an oversize drain line to the fixture as a drain. The extra diameter allows for proper air movement within the pipes without need of exterior venting. Or install an AAV at the fixture.

ACCORDING TO CODE

The minimum size of an individual vent line need be only half the required size of the fixture's drainpipe, but it can be no smaller than 1¼ in.

Locating the Vent

The ideal location for an individual vent is immediately behind the trap it is trying to protect.

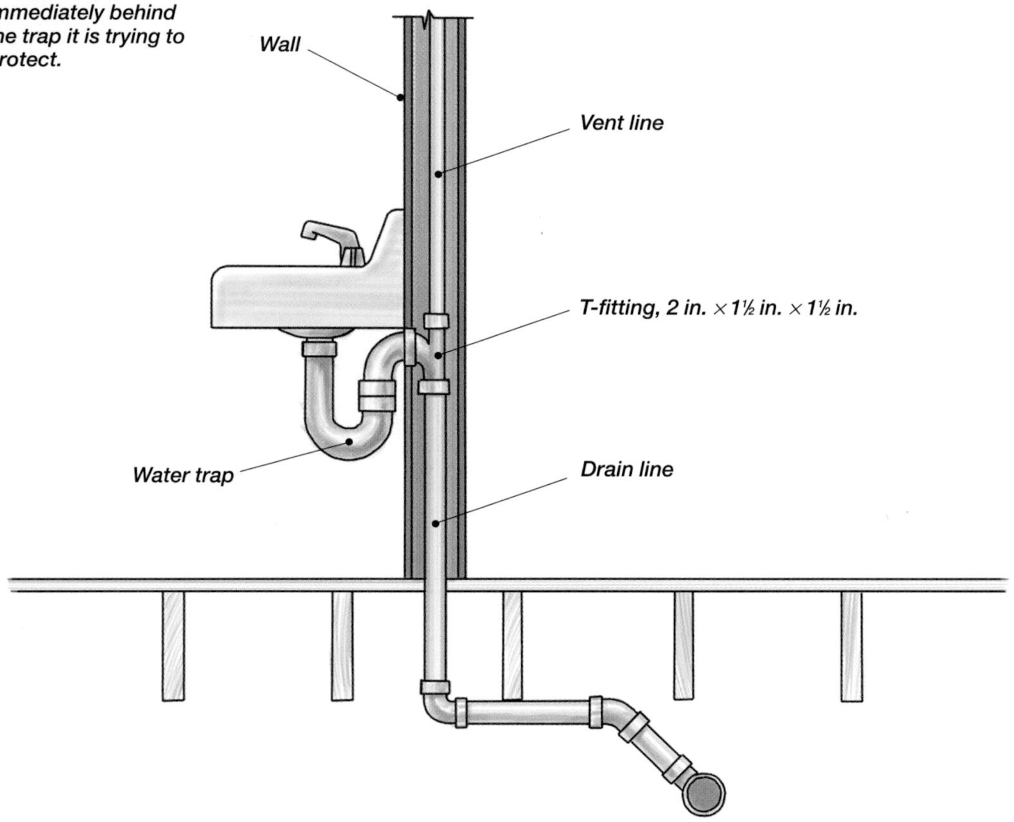

Wall

Vent line

T-fitting, 2 in. × 1½ in. × 1½ in.

Water trap

Drain line

Running Vent Pipe

Run individual vent pipe at least 6 in. above the flood rim of the sink before making the turn (top). This prevents its vent line from becoming blocked with sludge if the main sewer line downstream ever backs up (bottom).

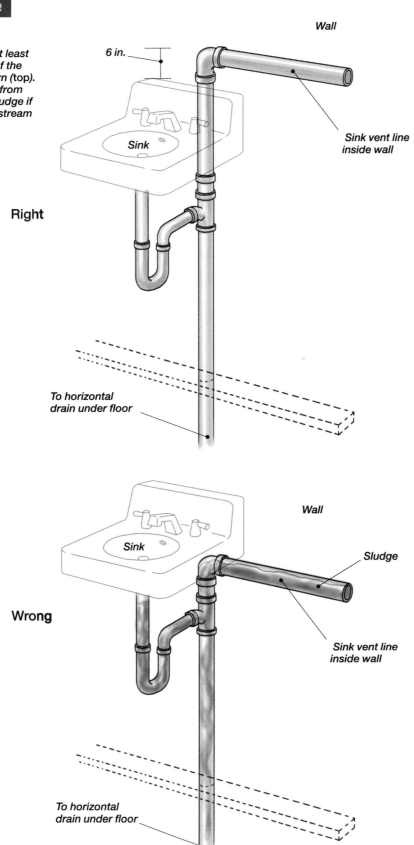

Wall

6 in.

Sink

Sink vent line
inside wall

Right

To horizontal
drain under floor

Sink

Wall

Sludge

Sink vent line
inside wall

Wrong

To horizontal
drain under floor

Venting Options

Oversize Line

If you cannot access the wall behind the trap, you can go a few feet downstream to add the vent line or make the line oversize for the fixture, as shown here.

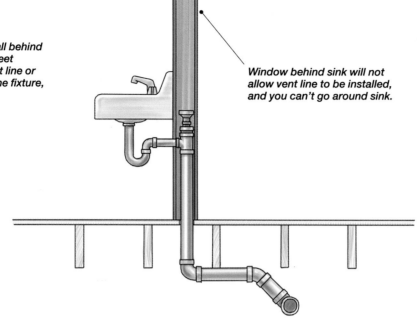

Window behind sink will not allow vent line to be installed, and you can't go around sink.

Individual AAV

For venting individual fixtures, air-admittance valves need to be installed immediately behind the trap, just before they enter the wall.

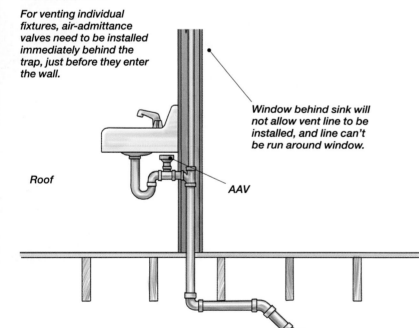

Window behind sink will not allow vent line to be installed, and line can't be run around window.

Roof

AAV

Ganged AAV

Air-admittance valves can vent several fixtures at once if brought together in the attic. Almost all codes allow the use of an AAV in lieu of an outside-air individual vent.

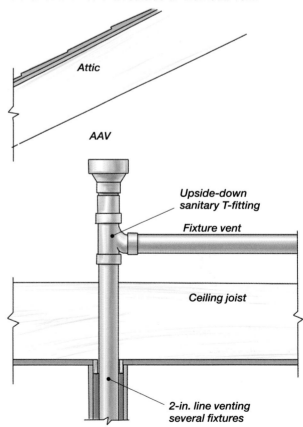

Attic

AAV

Upside-down sanitary T-fitting

Fixture vent

Ceiling joist

2-in. line venting several fixtures

Venting with AAVs

If you've ever looked under a sink or been in an attic and seen a plastic, white, mushroom-like object coming out of the drain line, it's probably an AAV, or air-admittance valve. An AAV is a handy alternative to a through-the-roof vent and can be a lifesaver for remodel work. However, check with your inspector before installing an AAV. Local codes may limit its use.

An AAV is a one-way air valve— meaning it lets fresh air come in, but does not let air go back out. It is used to vent a single fixture or group of fixtures. However, a home still needs at least one vent line extending outside. Here's how an AAV works: When negative air pressure accumulates inside the pipe to which it is attached, its valve door opens to admit air into the drain

lines. This prevents the water in the trap from being sucked out by a vacuum. AAVs are easier on your home's roof: You don't have to worry about a leak via roof penetration, and the roofer can put the roof on faster. You also don't have to cut holes between floors (ruining fire stops). I have used AAVs for many years without problems. Because of this, I rarely run an individual vent in a remodel.

As I noted, an AAV can serve as an individual vent for a single-plumbing fixture or as a group vent for several fixtures, including a complete add-on bath group. To vent a new sink with an AAV, bring the drain pipe out of the wall and into a 1½-in. T pointing straight up. Out of the top, install a short piece of pipe terminating in a female fitting. The AAV screws into that. Secure it with Teflon tape on the threads. The trap then connects to the front of the T-fitting. AAVs can also be installed both under the sink and in the wall immediately above the sink behind a louvered and accessible cover.

Do not confuse AAVs with low-cost, spring-operated automatic mechanical vents that sell for under $5; these are not up to code. If you decide to use an AAV for each fixture, remember that you still need a large-diameter main vent connecting to outside air for the drain system. (*Note:* AAVs only allow

Do Not Remove Sewer Vent

Air-admittance valves, an economical alternative to exterior vents, are ideal for remodels or first-floor plumbing projects.

air to enter; they do not allow air to leave.) For your system to breathe (air in and air out), it must be connected to outside air.

Here are some rules for AAVs:

■ They cannot be hidden or sealed within a wall cavity. They are allowed to be within a wall as long as the area around the vent is boxed off, accessible, and open to the inside of the house (like a laundry box with a louvered cover).

■ They must be installed vertically.

■ Unless otherwise approved, they can't take the place of the entire building's vent system. At some point, the vent system must be open to the atmosphere to let air in and out.

■ AAVs can only vent fixtures that are on the same floor.

■ AAVs must have ANSI/ASSE 1051 or 1050 (listing sticker) on them.

■ They cannot be buried in insulation.

■ The sealing membrane of an AAV has to be a minimum of 4 in. above the horizontal pipe to which it connects.

■ Always install the vent as close to the trap (downstream) as possible. Do not exceed the maximum trap-to-vent distance, typically 6 ft. to 8 ft. for 1½-in. to 2-in. pipe.

An AAV (*left*) is about the same height as a mechanical vent (*right*), but do not confuse the two.

Inside a mechanical vent is a spring, which is located over the top of the flapper.

Tapping In to Add Venting

If you are tapping into a horizontal line to add a vent, use a T-fitting turned on its back with the center inlet pointing up. If you need to make an immediate turn, use a street 90. It will act as a periscope and point any direction you want. If you need to go vertical before you go horizontal (when the main line is hanging low in the joists), simply add a vertical pipe and use a short-sweep 90 to make the overhead turn.

When adding a bathroom or plumbing group on the second floor, be sure to install a separate vent for the new group. The most common way to vent a new bath group is to run a new main vent to the outside and add individual vents or AAVs as required. It may be tempting to use the existing main vent of the first-floor plumbing for the new upstairs group; but if you do, the overburdened vent will underserve the first-floor bath group.

It's rare when a new-service drain line intersects the existing drain line at just the right angle so that the new pipe perfectly slides into the hub of a new tap fitting being cut into the old drain line. In other words, turns have to made. In addition to 90s and 45s, 60° and 22½° coupling-type fittings are available. With the variety of angle fittings available, you

Venting a Drain Line

Between Joists

Using a street 90 to swivel and point to the nearest wall is an easy way to vent a drain line.

Under Joists

If the pipe is lower than the joist, extend the inlet pipe vertically and use two 90s to get to the vent wall. Slope the horizontal vent line run as you would a drain line.

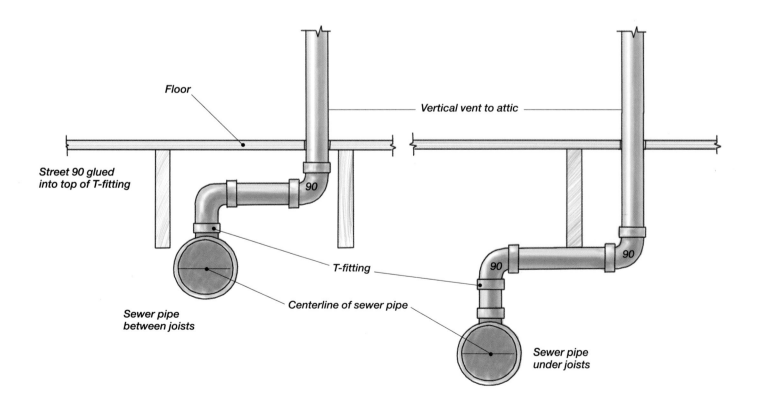

Floor

Vertical vent to attic

Street 90 glued into top of T-fitting

90

90

90

T-fitting

Centerline of sewer pipe

Sewer pipe between joists

Sewer pipe under joists

Getting the Dauber Size Right

The size of the dauber (glue applicator) should be appropriate for the pipe size. In one house, most of the drain system literally came apart and the entire system fell because all the large-diameter pipes pulled out of the hubs of the fittings. Upon investigation, I found that the person who plumbed the house (not a licensed plumber) used a small can of glue and a small dauber for both the large- and the small-diameter pipes. Small daubers cannot apply enough glue fast enough for large fittings and pipes before the glue starts to dry. In that house, what little glue was applied was almost dry before the pipe was inserted in the fitting.

Use a large dauber (*left*) to apply glue to the large-diameter pipe. If you use a small dauber (*right*), you may get poorly glued joints that come apart.

can get the new drain line close to the proper angle as you get ready to fit into a T- or Y-fitting on the main line.

For fine-tuning, use a Fernco or equivalent flexible coupling (or even a flexible elbow fitting) anywhere along the new drain line. These allow you to turn the pipe several degrees in any direction. Sometimes you have to install two such couplings, splitting a weird angle turn between them. Flexible elbows are wonderful fittings that allow significant changes in both a horizontal and a vertical direction. As an added bonus, they allow easy entry for rodding the lines.

COMMON VENTING PROBLEMS Often one drain line will develop air-pressure (or venting) problems. You can tell if a particular drain has problems by watching the toilet water when other fixtures are used in the house. The water in the bowl should not move as other toilets are flushed or other fixtures are used. In addition, when the clothes washer is pumping out water, it should not back up into any other appliance. Traps should not be pulled dry and no gurgling sound should be heard from the toilet or any other fixture.

Inadequate venting is a common problem. If you are adding a bath or

WHAT CAN GO WRONG

An old brass cleanout plug fastened to a rusted cast-iron fitting may cave in and crumple as you try to loosen it with a pipe wrench. To prevent this, heat the surrounding fitting with a propane torch to make it expand, and then try. As a last resort you may have to use a hammer and cold chisel on the threads to spin the plug off.

Code Requirements

▪ You need a minimum of 15 in. of space to both the left and the right of the toilet center, and more is better. You need 18 in. of clearance in front.

▪ A clothes washer can drain into an open laundry tub, but this will require approval by the local code official since he or she must verify that an air gap is present. In other words, do not just drop the hose into the tub. Support the hose so it will pour into the tub 1 in. or 2 in. above the flood rim.

▪ A common tub/shower is not always required to have a 2-in. drain line, but it is a good idea. A smaller drain line will clog faster from the oils and granular soaps used by some bathers (the oil coats the trap sides and the granular soap sticks to it). However, sometimes due to slope considerations only a 1½-in. pipe can be used. In these cases, attempt to keep the run as short as possible.

▪ Attempt to have at least one cleanout every 40 ft.—preferably at a fitting that has a major direction change.

▪ Minimum clearance behind a cleanout plug is normally 12 in. to 18 in. You need that much working space to rod the lines. This is occa-sionally overlooked by inspectors. You cannot seal a cleanout in a wall.

▪ Do not make an immediate turn down through the floor or wall, with the drain pipe, after a fixture trap. This makes an S-trap out of a P-trap. Behind the trap wier, go at least two pipe diameters horizon-tally first (approximately 3 in. for a 1½-in. pipe) before you turn down.

▪ Most codes require 4-in. sewer pipe after a third toilet is plumbed in. Thus, if your remodel will add a third toilet, be prepared to upgrade if all you have in-house is 3-in. pipe. This may be expensive if the 3-in. line extends out to the septic or town sewer.

▪ Vent lines have to be graded the same as common grade lines, but you can lower the slope from ¼ in. per foot to ⅛ in. per foot if you like. Remember to install vertical vent Ts backward (internal curve going up) so the air will flow smoother.

▪ Long-sweep elbows must be used where an upper floor intersects with a lower floor. You will typically install a cleanout at this point as well. It's a good policy to use long sweeps in place of short sweeps whenever possible.

other major plumbing appliance and there is only a single small pipe exiting the roof for a vent, there is not enough venting for the existing plumbing, much less for adding burdens to it. Thus do not tap into the existing venting for your new plumbing. Instead, add venting for the existing plumbing along with the venting for the new plumbing.

If the existing plumbing is quite old (steel pipes and cast iron) and there is minimal venting (one small pipe penetrating the roof), odds are there are additional problems caused by the old pipes being half full with crud (3-in. pipes may now have the usable diameter of a 1½-in. pipe). When this happens, very little vent air can travel over the water in the drain lines. You may need to replace (or a least clean) some of the old drain lines as well.

Choosing Fixture Location

Fixture location often determines how difficult the installation is going to be—and even whether a new fixture can be installed at all. If your home has an unfinished basement or a large crawl-space, your install work should be easy. As long as there is enough headroom to accommodate the required slope, you may be able to install new fixtures wherever you please.

If your home has minimal area under the floor joists to work with, your first choice for fixture location may not be worth the trouble of getting pipes to fit. Often moving a fixture a few feet can save a lot of work and money. In thinking through a proposed installation, ask these questions:

Wet Venting

A wet vent is a vent line that has drain water from another fixture running through it. This may or may not be allowed by code. It is tempting to install a wet vent when the pipe is already there and already going into the main drain line. If you do this, be sure that the wet vent fixtures are on the same floor and that the pipe diameter is at least 2 in., or at least one pipe size larger than minimum code.

The IPC allows a combination drain and vent system (Section 912). The number of fixtures in the system is unlimited as long as they are standpipes (clothes washer), emergency floor drains, and sinks (utility, kitchen, and bath). Simply increase the size of the drain pipe by around one size for air flow, which you should be doing anyway. This means no 1½-in. pipe. You must have at least one dry vent pipe (connected anywhere), or the system must be connected to a branch line that is vented.

- Is there enough vertical space to run the proposed drain line (traveling to the existing drain line) at the proper slope? Remember that the farther downstream you tap into the existing line, the more vertical space is needed.
- Will there be anything in the way of the proposed drain line?
- Will you be able to tap into the existing drain system at a spot that is significantly lower than where the remodel pipes will run down through the floor?
- If you cannot run pipes below joists, can you run them within the joist cavity, to minimize drilling and notching of joists? This is especially important for the toilet drain.
- Can you draw your plan on paper? It's important to visualize the pipes in place before you finalize your fixture locations. Base your plan on careful measurements. To gain perspective, use cardboard templates of the exact physical size of the fixtures going in. Don't forget which way the doors will swing.

Locating the Toilet Flange

Do not position the centerline of a toilet flange closer than 2½ in. from the edge of a joist. This position ensures that you won't have to cut the joist.

Toilet flange

Centerline

2½ in.

2½ in.

Floor joist

WHAT CAN GO WRONG

The two most common errors plumbers make in drain line installation are (1) inserting Ts and Ys in the backward position and (2) using short-sweep 90s.

Bathroom Sinks and Showers

A new bathroom sink can be added almost anywhere. Since the drain pipe exits the sink high, there is plenty of leeway for slope. Showers and tubs are another matter. Both require an accessible wall for the spigot, and both exit under the floor. Unless you are going to build a platform, you will need to have access underneath. If a platform will be built, allow for, as an absolute minimum, 5½ in. of clearance underneath (2x6). And don't forget about overhead clearance. A standing shower door is 6 ft. or more tall (and add a few inches for the base it sits on). A shower surround is 74 in. or more tall. Be sure there is enough vertical room. It might be tight if your basement is only 7 ft. Check out the Lasco door and surround that is only 66 in. tall for a neo standing shower.

Toilet Location

Choosing the location for a new toilet in a remodel situation requires extra thought for two reasons. First, the toilet must be positioned between floor joists, not on top of or even adjacent to the joists. In order for the toilet to fit between joists with enough clearance for the pipe and flanges, you need to know the exact location of the joists at the site. A subfloor should have a row of nails you can use to spot the joists. To determine whether the proposed toilet site will have sufficient clearance, drill a small pilot hole (¹⁄₁₆ in. or ⅛ in.) in the floor and poke a wire down. Look for the wire underneath, and check that you have 2½ in. of space around the wire for pipe and flange clearance. Do not consider using an offset flange (one that pulls the sewer line pipe to one side). You will have nothing but trouble because these do not allow the toilet to flush well.

Installing a Toilet Flange

Pick a flange. There are myriad flange types. I use a common plastic flange for 3-in. or 4-in. pipe that *does not* have a center knockout. I prefer flanges that are one piece (no moving parts) and that have U-shaped cutouts on each side. I avoid center knockouts because cutting them out adds to the workload. And I've had problems with removal (you sometimes have to use a jigsaw), breakage (that sends shards down the pipe), and jagged edges that can snag on toilet paper. To keep debris out of the hole, I cover the center hole with duct tape—no big deal.

Pick a bolt. Toilet bowl hold-down bolts are typically ¼ in. in diameter. I prefer the thicker ⁵⁄₁₆-in. bolt; it is much more secure. Wood screw–type bolts will secure the toilet bowl to a wood floor regardless of the condition of the flange.

Tighten the bolts onto the flange. I do not insert the bolts on the curved section of the flange because the bolts tend to spin as the nut is turned. Instead, I install the bolts in the U-shaped cutout where they can be locked tight via a washer and nut. Bolts secured this way cannot spin or be knocked over as you slide on the bowl.

Locate the flange installation site. A typical toilet rough-in center point is 12 in. from the finished wall. You will need at least 15 in. of elbow room both left and right of the toilet center and 18 in. in front. Make sure the flange is between the joists, and not on them. Drill a pilot hole if needed, stick down a wire, and check the location from underneath.

Determine the size hole your flange needs to sit flush to the floor, and use a compass to draw the proper diameter for cutting the circle.

Three flanges to avoid: offset (*left*), knockout (*right*), and small-diameter outlet (*bottom*).

It's best to secure the flange bolts (⁵⁄₁₆ in.) to the toilet flange via a ⁵⁄₁₆-in. nut and washer before installing the flange.

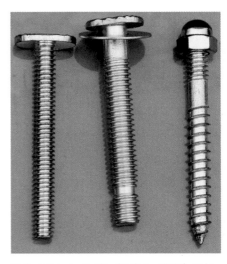

Toilet flange bolts (*left to right*): ¼ in. (most common), ⁵⁄₁₆ in. (preferred), and wood screw.

Cut open the hole, insert the flange, and attach it to the floor.

If a tile floor is to be installed, get a few pieces of the tile and insert then under the flange as a spacer. The tile installer will then remove the spacers and slip the tiles under as needed.

Installing a Toilet Flange

Mark a reference point 12½ in. out from the bottom plate (finished wall to be drywall). This will be used to draw a cutout circle, approximately 4½ in. in diameter.

Drill a ⅜-in. hole anywhere on the circular line.

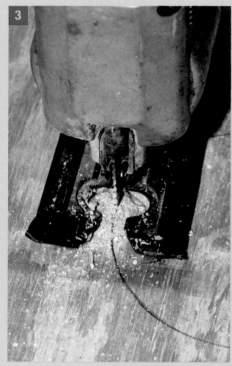

Using a jigsaw with a coarse blade, cut just to the outside of the line.

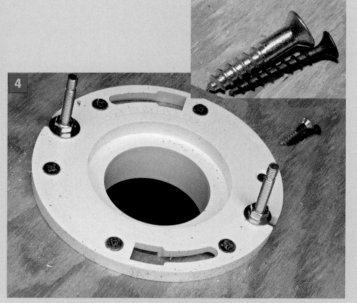

Insert the flange in the floor, align the flange bolts parallel to the floor plate, and secure with several 1¼-in. by #10 tapered-head wood screws (not drywall screws; their heads are too small).

If a slab is being poured, do not install the toilet flange until the slab is done. Just run the pipe up 1 ft. or 2 ft. above the propose slab top and cut it off flush with the slab later. Be sure to wrap some bubble wrap around the pipe where the slab meets the pipe. This will provide a gap between the concrete and pipe so the toilet flange can slide onto the pipe. Also, to get the precise location for the pipe, request a grade stake and an exact wall location. Once the pipe is set in concrete, the space behind has to be exactly 12 in. to the finished wall.

Under the Toilet Flange

The toilet line is always a tight fit between floor joists since the pipes take up so much room. A fitting under the flange needs 6 in. to 10 in. of clearance to make even a tight turn. After that, the line travels downhill at ¼ in. per foot toward a pipe that is at least 3 in. in diameter. Thus, if the line you want to tie into is 16 ft. away, you will need to drop 4 in. to get there, and if the line runs along the bottom of the joists, your new line may be too low to tie in once it gets there. In this case, you must do one of three things: tie into the existing line farther downstream, move the toilet closer to the existing line, or both. You will probably have to do both.

Working with a Finished Ceiling

If because of a finished ceiling below you have to keep the flange pipe within the floor joists, you will probably have to use a street 90. (The pipe-size end of the street 90 slips up into the hub of the closet flange.) Or you might use a short-sweep 90. As previously mentioned, short-sweep 90s are a last-resort choice since pipes that make sharp turns slow the fluid down and are more prone to

Locating the Sewer Pipe

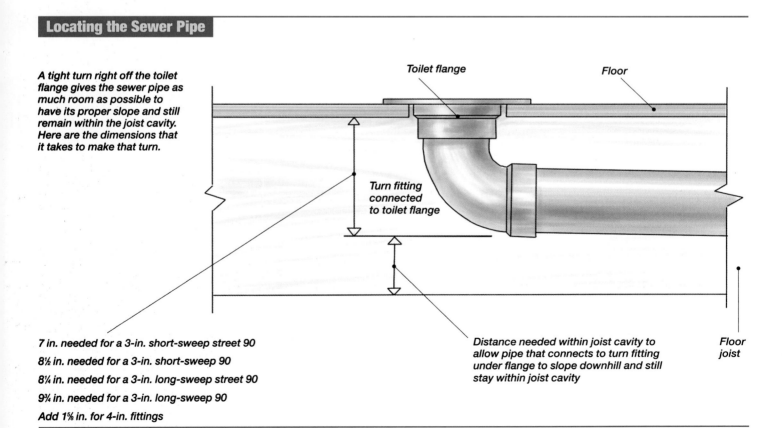

A tight turn right off the toilet flange gives the sewer pipe as much room as possible to have its proper slope and still remain within the joist cavity. Here are the dimensions that it takes to make that turn.

Toilet flange

Floor

Turn fitting connected to toilet flange

7 in. needed for a 3-in. short-sweep street 90
8½ in. needed for a 3-in. short-sweep 90
8¼ in. needed for a 3-in. long-sweep street 90
9¾ in. needed for a 3-in. long-sweep 90
Add 1⅝ in. for 4-in. fittings

Distance needed within joist cavity to allow pipe that connects to turn fitting under flange to slope downhill and still stay within joist cavity

Floor joist

■ **WORK SAFE**
■ **WORK SMART**

The best place for the main house cleanout (and every house needs one so the main line run can be rodded if need be) is outside. It is easier to get to and far less messy than having it inside.

Turning Corners

Gentle angles are always best for turning corners. A soft-angle turn slows fluids less and allows for easier rodding of the lines. A soft angle also sidesteps codes that may require a cleanout at every bend with an angle sharper (more) than 45°. Of the fittings made to turn corners (22½, 45, 60, and 90), the one to avoid whenever possible is perhaps the one most used: the 90. Instead of a 90, you can use two 45 fittings separated by a piece of pipe (the longer the better). If a 90 fitting is unavoidable (and many times they are), use a long-sweep 90 rather than a short one. Use the short-sweep 90 as a last resort, when you have no other choice due to slope or clearance problems, such as working within joist cavities above finished ceilings.

When possible, use rigid fittings in angles less than 90° to turn corners. Fittings for angles of 22½°, 45°, and 60° are available.

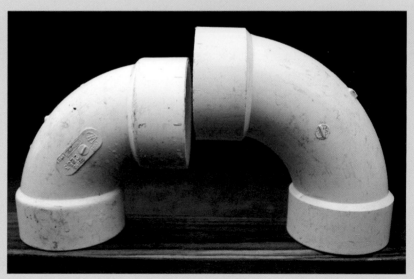

A long-sweep 90 (*right*) is 1 in. longer (or taller) than a short-sweep 90 (*left*).

Making Turns with Street Fittings

I don't know how these fittings got their name. But a street fitting is an angle fitting (such as a 45 or 90) that has a hub on one end and an angled pipe on the other. Use them when you want to make a turn as fast as possible when coming out of another hub-type fitting. For example, say you have a T-fitting resting on its back center with the T pointing up. If you insert a street 90 into its center inlet, you will have a periscope fitting that you can swivel in any direction. If you insert a street 45 into the center hub of a Y-fitting, you will have a T/Y-combo; the Y-fitting will now have a center outlet to accepts pipe that runs parallel to the main pipe line. A T/Y-combo is always preferred over a T because, when fluids are flowing in the line, it doesn't disrupt the flow as a T-fitting might.

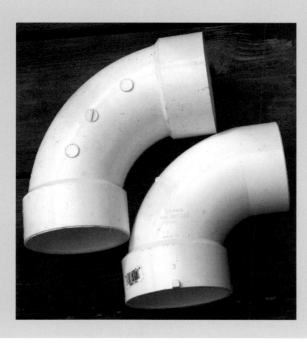

Compared to a common 90 (*left*), which has a hub on both ends, a street fitting (*right*) has an OD at one end that matches the OD of the pipe.

ACCORDING TO CODE

Cleanouts concealed behind permanent obstructions are inaccessible and may not be counted as a required cleanout. Removable panels are okay.

■ WORK SAFE
■ WORK

Try to avoid immediate-turn 90° fittings. Rodding equipment is not flexible enough for sharp turns, and turns softer than 90° aren't required to have a cleanout. When possible, use a 45 and then go a short distance and install another 45. If you have to use a 90, attempt to use a long sweep first; use the short-sweep 90 only as a last resort.

clogging, but sometimes there is no other alternative.

Running Lines below the Joists

If headroom is not a problem and you are able to run new lines below the joists, start the new run by inserting vertically into the flange a section of pipe that is long enough to extend below the floor joists. It should end up low enough so that there will be room above the pipe for vent takeoffs and taps for other fixtures.

Connecting the Sewer Line

If you are running pipes under joists, there are three ways to connect to the sewer line.

Common Method

The most common way to attach to a sewer line is to glue a vertical extension pipe into the flange and use 45° fittings and Y-fittings to connect to the main sewer line.

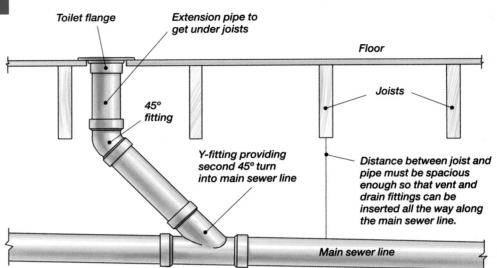

Toilet flange

Extension pipe to get under joists

Floor

45° fitting

Joists

Y-fitting providing second 45° turn into main sewer line

Distance between joist and pipe must be spacious enough so that vent and drain fittings can be inserted all the way along the main sewer line.

Main sewer line

Faster Method

A faster method is to use a Y-fitting with a street 45 fitting glued into its inlet to make the overhead connection.

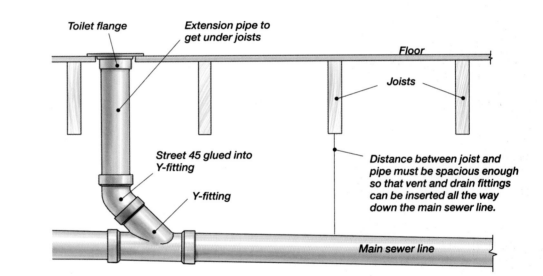

Toilet flange

Extension pipe to get under joists

Floor

Joists

Street 45 glued into Y-fitting

Y-fitting

Distance between joist and pipe must be spacious enough so that vent and drain fittings can be inserted all the way down the main sewer line.

Main sewer line

Fastest Method

A still faster method is to use a T/Y-combo fitting.

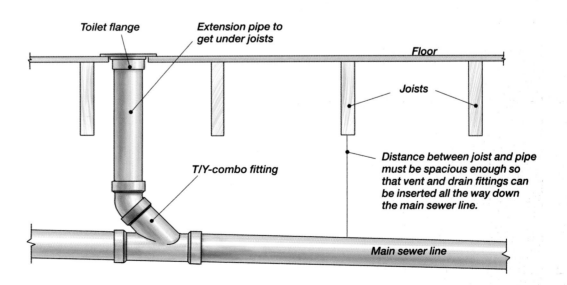

Toilet flange

Extension pipe to get under joists

Floor

Joists

T/Y-combo fitting

Distance between joist and pipe must be spacious enough so that vent and drain fittings can be inserted all the way down the main sewer line.

Main sewer line

Fittings and Methods

Well, now it's time to get dirty. You're going to be cutting holes (wear safety glasses) and perhaps even going into the crawlspace. If so, don't crawl in the dirt. Lay down cardboard, plywood, or carpet runners. Carpet remnants are great. Now, step back and take a look at the overall picture, make sure you know what is going to happen, assemble all your tools and fittings, take a deep breath, and get going.

Order of Work

First, visually check your fixture and drain locations to be sure they will work. Sometimes I cut out cardboard templates and lay them out. Once all proposed fixture locations are known, drill a pilot hole through the floor at each proposed drain location and stick a wire down. Go under the floor and look at all the wires to be sure there are no obstacles in the paths where pipes will run when connecting to the new or old lines; for example, piers and ductwork. In addition, verify that there is enough headroom for slope requirements. Visualize which pipe is going where, and make a mental list of the fittings you will need.

Next, cut the floor holes for the drain pipes. The best tool for cutting is a hole saw used with a right-angle drill. A jigsaw or reciprocating saw will work fine, too. A large-diameter hole saw is also good for cutting holes for toilet flanges, but the extreme cost may not be justified for a single small project.

Once the holes are cut, you're ready to begin running new pipe to the main line.

Save the work of cutting into the existing drain line for last. Why? Because as soon as you cut into the old drain line, the sewer gas in the lines will escape and the pipe will start dripping. Be sure to place a cap on the end of the new pipe coming up from the floor plate to contain the fumes once you join the new pipe to the drain line.

Before you cut the existing sewer/drain lines do the following:

- Arrange for house inhabitants to go elsewhere for a few hours while you work on the lines. If that is not possible, take the next precautions.
- Notify all in the house not to use any water, especially the toilets.
- Turn off the house water.
- Flush all toilets that might flow through the line you are cutting.
- If there are kids in the house, close the toilet lids and secure them with duct tape; affix a note that says: "Do not use." Bottom line: You can't be too careful on this part of the project.

Tips for Making Connections

When attaching new tap fittings (Ts, Ys, T/Y-combos) to the existing main pipe line, be sure the center inlet of the interface fitting is positioned (by swiveling it) at least 45° up from the horizontal position. This keeps fluid that's flowing down the larger pipe from entering the drain line of another pipe. And if the smaller pipe is serving as a vent, the fluid won't block the air off from the vent line. *Whenever fluid from the tap line runs into the main line*, the interface fitting should be, if possible, a Y or T/Y-combo (the combo is a Y with a ⅛ bend; it looks like a long-sweep T), as opposed to a common sanitary T. This is code in most areas (officially, a T-fitting on its back is not a drain fitting), but the rule has been deleted by at least one jurisdiction. Many code inspectors are not even aware of the rule's existence because they have seen and installed Ts on their backs all their lives (and I've done it as well), and the inspectors know this setup will work just fine.

■ **WORK SAFE**
■ **WORK SMART**

To avoid getting a shock, power your AC tools via a ground-fault circuit interrupter (GFCI) or use cordless tools.

ACCORDING TO CODE

You are not allowed to drill into a drain pipe and insert a drain hose—as is commonly done for the high-pressure discharge of a water

ACCORDING TO CODE

You are not allowed to tap into a drain line by drilling a hole in the pipe. A fitting called a saddle is sometimes used (sometimes not), but this is not approved by all codes.

Controlling Air

Laying a T-fitting on its side will invite the fitting to fill with fluid, blocking off air from the outside and creating positive and negative pressures within the drain system.

Vent line

Air in vent line at atmospheric pressure

Fluid in pipe blocking off air from vent line to drain line

Centerline

■ **WORK SAFE**
■ **WORK SMART**

Have a fan ready to turn on when you cut into the sewer line. The fan will blow away the smelly sewer gas so you can work.

The problem is not that they don't work, but that they can disrupt the flow of the fluid within the pipe, lowering the flow velocity below 2 ft. per second so that solids come out of suspension. It is true that a sanitary T will direct the flow slightly in its intended direction as it comes into the main line, but not nearly as well as a Y-fitting. The Y or T/Y-combo will direct the fluid from the tap line into the main line at a 45° angle, which allows the fluid to travel at a high velocity as it enters the main line and continue that way in the main line. By contrast, a sanitary T directs the fluid into the main line in nearly a straight line, which slows the flow in the tap line and disrupts the flow in the main line, slowing its flow as well.

The bottom line is: Use a sanitary T only as a last resort when space constraints offer no other choice, and be aware it is against code in most areas. However, using a T on its back as a vent in this position is just fine and, in fact, is recommended. Use a street 90 in the inlet and point the 90 toward the incoming tap line. The 90 acts like a little periscope that can point any direction.

When adding a small drain line with a long run, the slope requirement (1 in. per 4 ft.) often brings the pipe down so low it's hard to tap into the main line (because it may be higher). You may be tempted to raise the long-run tap line pipe and reduce the slope. Though a slope of ⅛ in. per foot is well within code, it may lower the velocity of the fluid, which may mean backup problems down the road (but, if you have to do it, you have to do it). A slope of ¹⁄₁₆ in. per foot will be passed by most inspectors but almost guarantees future problems. This is why you should always run the large main line pipe 1 ft. or 2 ft. below the joists, if possible.

To give a new line the proper slope without excessively lowering the main line, run the tap line parallel to and between the joists, if possible. If your

The Y-fitting (*left*) and T/Y-combo (*right*) are the two preferred fittings for bringing fluids into a main line.

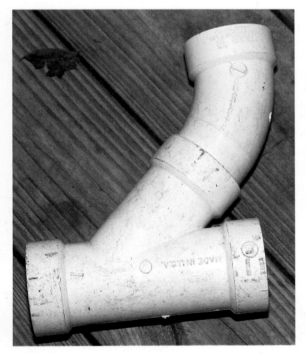

Inserting a street 45 into a Y-fitting creates the same angle as a T/Y-combo.

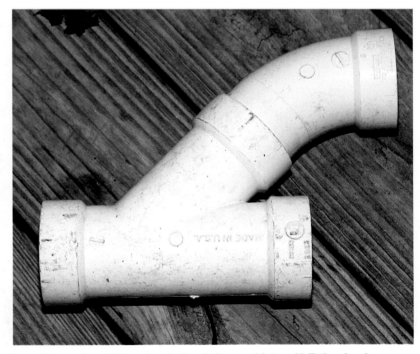

Inserting a street 45 and pointing it forward into a Y-fitting is also acceptable and takes up less headroom.

■ **WORK SAFE**
■ **WORK SMART**

Have all fittings and tools available at arm's length when you cut into the sewer line. The faster you do the work the less sewer gas you will have to deal with.

■ **WORK SAFE**
■ **WORK SMART**

Resist the urge to smoke while cutting into a sewer line. Sewer gas is highly flammable.

Smooth Flow

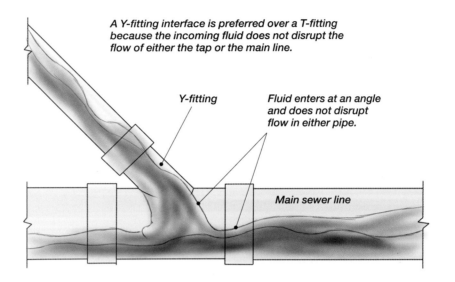

A Y-fitting interface is preferred over a T-fitting because the incoming fluid does not disrupt the flow of either the tap or the main line.

Y-fitting

Fluid enters at an angle and does not disrupt flow in either pipe.

Main sewer line

Drilling Joists

Whenever possible, run the drain and sewer lines without drilling into the joists. It's faster, and you don't have to worry about compromising structural integrity. However, there may be occasions when you simply have to go through the joist to get into an adjacent cavity. When this happens, be careful to drill through the joist center only, and drill a hole no larger than one-third of the joist width. Thus, for a 2x10 joist, you would be limited to a 2-in. pipe. If you have no choice but to run 3-in. pipe through a joist, you must reinforce the joist with a steel plate or the equivalent to compensate for the loss of structural integrity—and you may have to install steel plates along the edge of the joist to prevent screws and nails from damaging the pipe. If you are on a job site, do not do this unless you have the lead carpenter's permission.

joists are 2x10, you'll have 9¼ in. of leeway before the new pipes reach the bottom of the joists. Of course, this is possible only if the joists run parallel to the direction of the new pipes. When you have a long run from the kitchen (and the run is at an angle to the joists), you can slightly notch joists at the beginning of the kitchen drain line run. This allows the pipe to start at a higher elevation. You are normally allowed to notch 1½ in. into a 2x10. If you are on a job where there is a master or lead carpenter, ask him or her before you notch the joist. This will endear you to him or her forever. Notch each joist as the line lowers 1 in. every 4 ft. In a few feet you should be flush with the bottom of the joists. This may not solve the entire problem, but it will give you some extra headroom you didn't have before.

Velocity of Flow

Directing the flow of the fluid into the main drain line at an angle (via a Y-fitting or T/Y-combo fitting) maintains velocity and ensures the flow in the main line is not disrupted.

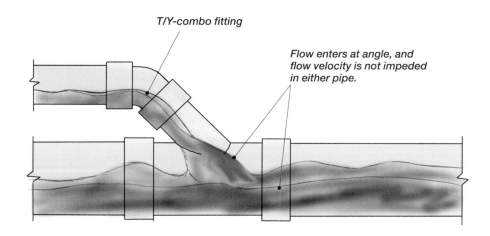

T/Y-combo fitting

Flow enters at angle, and flow velocity is not impeded in either pipe.

Disrupted Flow

Directing the fluid into the main line via a T-fitting will work but may disrupt the flow in both lines.

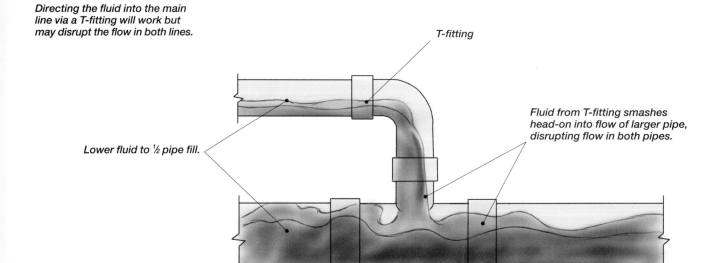

T-fitting

Lower fluid to ½ pipe fill.

Fluid from T-fitting smashes head-on into flow of larger pipe, disrupting flow in both pipes.

Working with Minimal Crawlspace

Running pipe through a tiny crawlspace is always a problem, but with a little forethought and luck it can be done. Two things need to happen. First, you need access to where the new line ties into the old line; in other words, you need lots of working room. If this is not available, you may have to dig out the area to create more space. Second, check to see which way the floor joists run. If they run in a line to where the new line ties into the old line, you might be able to squeeze a drain pipe over the dirt and between floor joists. If the joists run at 90° to where you want to tie in, you will need clearance under the joists to install the new pipe with the proper slope. If the clearance isn't there, you (or perhaps a young person willing to do grunt work) will need to dig out the area to provide sufficient space.

To prepare the fixture site for the installation, remove a small piece of flooring between two joists where the fixture or appliance will be installed. The cutout area should be large enough to accommodate the person who will be reaching into the cavity to find the pipe as it is being pushed in from the opposite end. Remember that the proposed pipe in the crawlspace needs to be installed in a straight path from the proposed fixture location to the open crawlspace.

Prepare the pipe. On one end of a long section of pipe, friction-fit a cap to keep out debris as the pipe is being pushed under the house. This cap will be removed once the pipe has been pushed under the house. Approximately every 4 ft. along the length of the pipe, attach treated lumber blocks to the bottom of the pipe to obtain the desired slope.

The starting point for attaching blocks will be 4 ft. back (not at the cap). For example, you'll first attach three stacked 2x4 blocks of treated lumber 4 ft. from the cap; then 4 ft. down the pipe, you'll attach two stacked blocks; then in another 4 ft. you'll attach one block. To hold the blocks in place, you can use stainless-steel clamps or tightly wrapped duct tape. If there is a hump in the dirt floor under the joist, you may have to leave off one or more blocks.

From the open crawlspace area, determine which joist cavity you need to be in, lay the pipe sideways, and push the pipe all the way to the opposite end to where the opening has been cut. Once the pipe is in place, turn it up so the pipe is lying on the blocks. On the open crawlspace side, you might be able to reach in with a shovel to dig out some dirt under the pipe to provide some downward slope at that point. This system works well; I have done it many times.

The diameter of the pipe needs to be a minimum of 2 in. However, 3 in. would be better; because the pipe is resting on uneven ground, it may not have the proper continuous slope from beginning to end and you don't have access for hanging it properly. Consequently, there may be some water that doesn't drain out of the pipe and, over time, the pipe will tend to clog. A larger-diameter pipe will be less likely to clog. A 3-in. pipe also has fewer venting problems (for instance, siphoning out a trap) since there is a large air cavity over the water flow. However, if your pipe is smaller, you can always run a vent line or install an AAV.

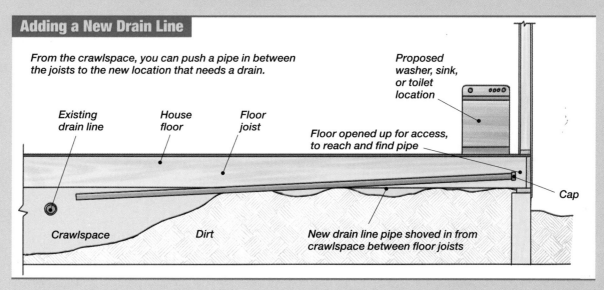

Adding a New Drain Line

From the crawlspace, you can push a pipe in between the joists to the new location that needs a drain.

Proposed washer, sink, or toilet location

Existing drain line *House floor* *Floor joist*

Floor opened up for access, to reach and find pipe

Cap

Crawlspace *Dirt* *New drain line pipe shoved in from crawlspace between floor joists*

Notching a Floor Joist

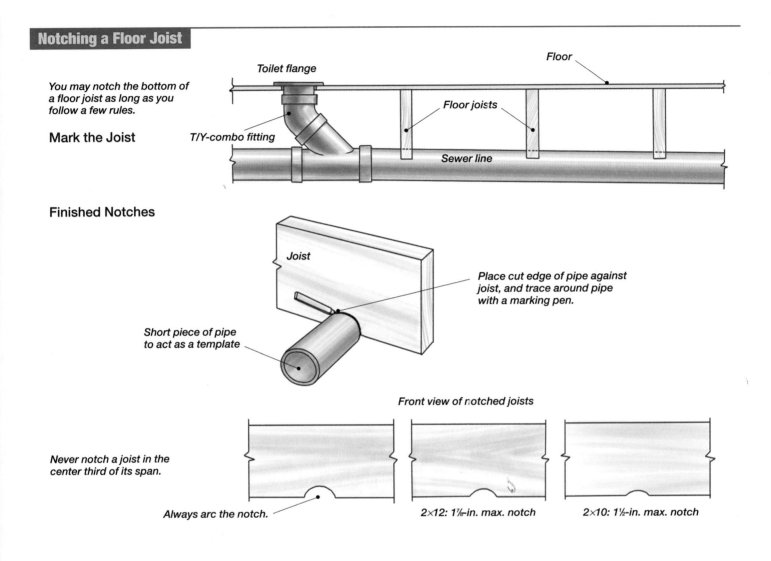

You may notch the bottom of a floor joist as long as you follow a few rules.

Mark the Joist

Floor

Toilet flange

T/Y-combo fitting

Floor joists

Sewer line

Finished Notches

Joist

Place cut edge of pipe against joist, and trace around pipe with a marking pen.

Short piece of pipe to act as a template

Front view of notched joists

Never notch a joist in the center third of its span.

Always arc the notch.

2×12: 1⅞-in. max. notch

2×10: 1½-in. max. notch

Cutting into the Lines

Before cutting in to the lines, be sure you know what type of pipe you will be cutting into: Will it be plastic, cast iron, copper, or steel? Plastic, either white PVC or black ABS, is easiest to work with, although ABS tends to melt back together if you let it. That is, the small plastic cut pieces will remelt back into the gap that was cut. To cut either, use a PVC/ABS handsaw or a reciprocating saw. I have also drilled a starter hole in plastic pipe and then cut around the pipe with a jigsaw. Copper is also easy to cut; I use a reciprocating saw equipped with a long, fine-toothed blade.

Steel lines are normally run in combination with cast iron pipes. Typically the larger 3-in. and 4-in. lines are made of cast iron, and the smaller 2-in. and 1½-in. lines are steel. It's easy to cut steel pipe using either a reciprocating saw or a circular saw with a metal-cutting blade. However, cutting through 3-in. and 4-in. cast-iron pipe is another story.

WORK SMART

If you want to reuse a fitting that was cut out of the drain line or a fitting that is still on the drain line, be sure to leave enough pipe attached to the fitting to permit you to slide on a coupling (or another fitting).

Drilling Holes

Whenever possible, a hole drilled through a stud or joist for should exceed the outer diameter of the pipe by ⅛ in. to ¼ in. This slightly enlarged size prevents squeaking (rubbing against the wood) as the pipe expands and contracts. Typically, the outer diameter of a drain pipe is ½ in. larger than the inner diameter.

Pipe and Hole Diameters

Pipe Diameter	Hole Diameter
1½ in.	2¼ in.
2 in	2¾ in.
3 in.	3¾ in.
4 in.	4¾ in.

WORK SAFE
WORK SMART

Be sure to wear eye protection, gloves, and a long-sleeve shirt when cutting into a cast-iron line.

WORK SAFE
WORK SMART

Cutting into an old sewer line can be messy work. Have handy some towels and antiseptic mouth wash to use for washing your hands when you are done.

The easiest way to cut already-installed cast iron is with a circular saw (with a solid blade). However, for this you'll need a large open area around the pipe. You won't be able to cut the pipe like you would a board since the blade is not large enough in diameter, so you'll have to circle around it. And then you may need to finish the job using a 4½-in. small-angle grinder (with a metal-cutting blade). You could also rent a pipe snapper. I have often misused my 14-in. solid-blade cutoff saw by holding it up against the pipe to be cut and then cutting the pipe as if with a chopsaw. I saw one person with infinite patience use a drill to make a hundred ¼-in. holes around the pipe, then snap it with a sharp hammer blow. Bottom line: A lot depends on the available working space and what seems easiest for each particular job.

Hanging the Pipe

Don't underestimate the importance of proper technique for hanging pipe. I say this because many plumbers have totally screwed up a job by improperly hanging pipe. Properly hung pipe provides the slope you need; without proper slope, you don't have a drain system. It is the strapping that determines the slope. On one competitor's job, the entire drain system broke free and fell, turning the entire crawlspace into a septic tank for several months. You can design the best system in the world and use the best materials; but if it isn't hung right, nothing will work right.

Use Galvanized Strapping

There are many types of strapping available: copper coated, thin galvanized, thick galvanized, ungalvanized, plastic hooks, and perhaps even others. However, I use nothing but thick galvanized strapping. It's economical and works well, so why change? Attach the strapping to the joists using a cordless drill and 5⁄16 in. hex-head sheet-metal-type screws. This method provides great flexibility because the hex head allows you to quickly install or remove screws for fine-tuning—to move the pipe left or right for the proper angle as well as up and down for slope. Never use nails. Nails cannot be easily withdrawn for minor changes of slope or change of pipe directions.

MATERIALS TO AVOID I do not recommend plastic strapping for drain and sewer lines (except for temporary use) because it stretches over time—the pipe is heavy, and even heavier with water in it—and can break. Ungalvanized strapping rusts and breaks. I also avoid plastic J-hooks for hanging drain pipe. They are expensive, and I worry that they may snap if the pipe gets bumped. Be wary of small-diameter hex-head screws. The heads snap off very easy. That's why I use ⁵⁄₁₆ in.

Strapping Methods

Strap drain and sewer pipe at least every 3 ft. to 4 ft. and at each location where the pipe branches off. If strapping intervals exceed 4 ft., the pipe may sag between straps and collect sludge. This is especially common for lines that carry very hot water, like the kitchen drain. The fastest method (when running parallel to the joists) is to hang a single strap from joist to joist like a horseshoe with the pipe in the center or, if you are running at an angle with the joists, hang the strap directly down from the joist. Another good method is to wrap the strapping around the pipe and connect both ends to the joist with ⁵⁄₁₆ in. hex-head screws. Whichever method you use, cut the strapping to include a generous margin of several inches for up-and-down adjustment if needed.

For very long runs and for hanging pipe that will be bumped by items being stored nearby, I first use strapping to hang the pipe and get the proper slope. Then I use 2x4 material to form a cradle around the pipe every 3 ft. to 4 ft.

Install in Two Phases

Strapping work is typically done in two phases—rough and finish. First, strap the pipe where you think it should go, roughly guessing at the slope and getting it close to where you want the pipe run. Then stand back and take a look. Is this the best route for the pipe? Is it the proper slope? If you think everything is going to work, start the finish work by moving things around to get slope and location as exact as you can. Then start gluing the pipe.

Don't forget that common wood blocks between joists can support drain pipe as well.

Drain Line Design Checklist

- ■ Are the Ts, Ys, and T/Y-combos installed facing the right way?
- ■ Are the vent Ts installed upside down as they should be?
- ■ Do you have a minimum slope on all drain lines?
- ■ Did you use large enough pipe?
- ■ Did you stay within the maximum distance limits for fixture to vent?
- ■ Did you always keep the sink's vertical vent takeoff above the trap's weir?
- ■ Did you run the sink's vertical vent line above the overflow lip of the sink before you went horizontal with the vent line?
- ■ Are cleanouts installed with proper clearance behind?
- ■ Are the pipe's strapped properly?
- ■ If required, is fire stop caulk installed around the pipe (sealing the gap between the pipe and wood) between floors?

Tapping into an Existing Drain Line

Using a Flexible T-Fitting

It is possible to tap into a rigid drain line using a flexible T-fitting.

Step 1

Place flexible fitting parallel to pipe where fitting is needed. Mark pipe where inside of flexible fitting hub meets pipe.

Step 2

Cut pipe to the outside of mark and remove section.

Step 3

Remove clamps, squeeze flexible fitting together, and insert into cut area. Orient fitting, reinstall clamps, and tighten.

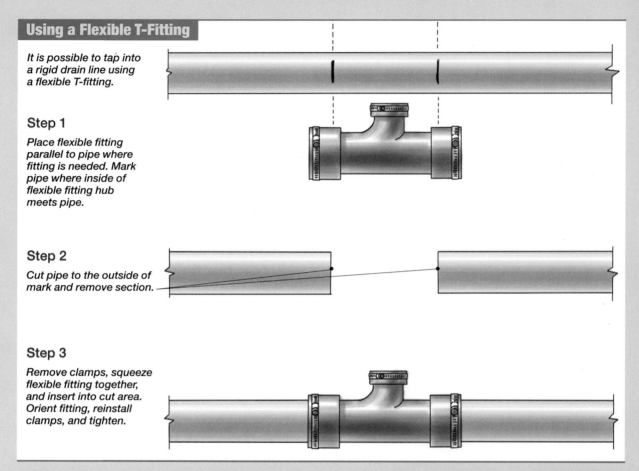

Flexible fittings are great for remodel work since they can be inserted easily into existing rigid drain lines.

Using a Tap Fitting

It is possible to tap into a rigid drain line using a rigid pipe and flexible couplings, or a tap fitting assembly.

Step 1

First, create a tap fitting assembly by gluing two short pipes into each end of a Y-fitting (or T-fitting).

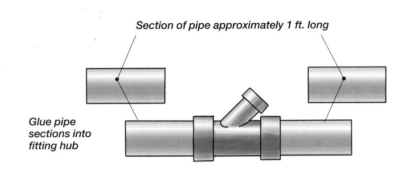

Section of pipe approximately 1 ft. long

Glue pipe sections into fitting hub

Step 2

Place the tap fitting assembly parallel to the existing pipe run. Mark the existing pipe at each end of the assembly. (The section between these marks will be cut out to make room for the assembly.)

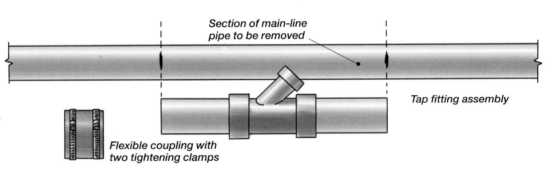

Section of main-line pipe to be removed

Tap fitting assembly

Flexible coupling with two tightening clamps

Step 3

Cut and remove the marked section from the pipe. Loosen the clamps and slide the flexible couplings onto the cut pipe ends.

Step 4

Insert the tap fitting assembly between the pipe run ends. Center the flexible couplings over the cuts (sliding them into place). Orient the pipe and assembly and tighten the clamps.

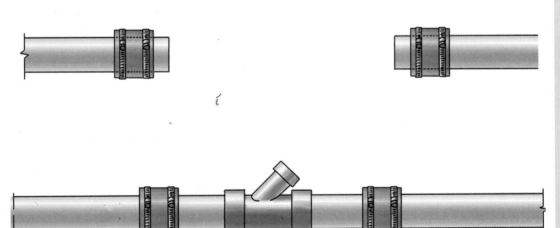

CHAPTER 4

Remodeling the Kitchen

N THE PAST FEW decades, the kitchen has grown both in physical size and functional versatility. It has become for many, more of a family room than the family room itself—a favorite gathering place. Kitchen appliances have also evolved, from basic utilitarian units to smart, good-looking elements in the kitchen's design. A kitchen remodel can be fun because it removes the old, leaking, boring kitchen of the past and replaces it with a modern, ultra-functional, eye-appealing space that is a pleasure to use.

Even a high-end kitchen upgrade does not usually require a lot of complicated plumbing work. This chapter will walk you through several real-life plumbing projects—from the modest to the expansive—common to kitchen remodel jobs.

Some of these projects make kitchen plumbing operate smoothly and efficiently. Others include appliance installa-

This custom copper-beaten sink is a piece of art that brings back memories of yesteryear.

tion, and step-by-step information is provided to help you calculate space requirements, remove the old appliance, and install the new. This chapter also includes helpful shortcuts and tips for avoiding errors made by me and others, so your remodel job will go smoothly.

The Kitchen Sink

I remember the first sink I helped my uncle Bud install when I was a child. It was cast iron and as heavy as can be. My finger got squished under the lip as we set it into the countertop cutout. I've not made that mistake again.

Today, bright colors (even splatters) are popular elements of kitchen design, and often the kitchen sink is the star of the show. I've noticed that most people who have lived with a low-cost sink for a long time don't mind spending money for a better one. In fact, during a remodel, the kitchen sink is normally the first thing to go. So for our first plumbing project, we are replacing a shallow and stained stainless-steel sink with a newer, more interesting model.

We will also replace the old faucet; 9 times out of 10 this is replaced along with the sink. Homeowners tend to pick what looks good, but plumbers know which faucets work well and which don't.

(*Note*: Plumbers typically say: "Order any faucet you want, as long as it is a [fill in their favorite brand]" because they don't want to get saddled with a faucet that is hard to install and that doesn't work well. And they don't want to have to explain later why a faucet they didn't want to install to begin with has begun to leak.)

For this job, we will replace the sink strainers, too, because they are part of the "ugly" problem and often leak. And we

Picking a Stainless-Steel Sink

Stainless steel is the most common sink choice. Look for a sink with a solid, heavy feel, constructed of thick metal, as indicated by a lower gauge number—for example, 18 as opposed to 22. The thicker the metal, the higher the price, but you get what you pay for. A thicker sink will vibrate less and will be less likely to bend as you twist the faucet head. Avoid the cheapest models at all costs.

To eliminate problems with surface rust and staining, choose a sink with at least 10 percent nickel in the metal. Most low-end sinks have 8 percent, and these are the sinks that develop surface rust. A sink rated 18/10 (meaning 18-gauge thickness and 10 percent nickel content) is a good choice.

Also, look for ample soundproofing on the underside of the sink. Better sinks are coated on the underside with spray-on soundproofing. Low-cost sinks have either a tiny foam pad stuck to the underside of each bowl instead of a coating or nothing. However, there is no reason you can't buy a can of car undercoating and spray under the bowl yourself.

Some high-end sinks have a mirror finish, which means they have had an extra buffing to make them shine more. This is a matter of taste.

will reconfigure the under-sink plumbing to move drain lines back from the center of the cabinet, so cabinet space will be more usable.

Decisions, Decisions

Moderately priced sinks are in the $300 range, and low-end sinks are in the $100 range. Avoid the lowest-priced sinks because they tend to develop cosmetic problems quickly. High-end sinks are often stunning, but so are their price tags. In this remodel, we want to brighten up the kitchen at a moderate price, so we will install a midprice colored sink. If you prefer stainless steel, see "Picking a Stainless-Steel Sink" above. For a discussion of options in sink materials (such as acrylic, enamel on steel, and composite), see "What Sinks Are Made Of" on p. 102. Always choose a

What Sinks Are Made Of

Kitchen sinks can be constructed from many different materials, and prices vary widely. Each material has its faults and benefits. A photograph in a catalog will not give you a reliable impression of a sink. Visit a showroom or home center, so you can touch as well as see your options.

Stainless Steel

Stainless steel is the most popular sink material installed. Both quality and price ($30 to $1,000 and up) vary considerably. For more information, see "Picking a Stainless-Steel Sink" on p. 101.

Enameled

Enamel-on-steel is low cost ($100 and up) and can look shiny and beautiful, at least when you first buy it. It looks like cast iron but weighs a lot less. However, it chips easily if something heavy hits it, it's likely to lose its shine after a few years, and the enamel can wear away in spots after a decade or so. This type of sink was common in early mobile homes.

Cast Iron

Cast-iron sinks have a porcelain enamel coating over a base of very heavy cast iron. The mainstay of early plumbing, they are now making a comeback in some areas. Cast-iron sinks are beautiful and can stay so for a lifetime. The porcelain coating retains its shine for decades, and it is much more resistant to chipping than an enamel-on-steel sink. However, the enamel can chip or crack if it gets banged with a heavy pan. To be safe, set a mat in the sink bottom. You will guarantee a chip (or popout) if you set a hot cast-iron skillet directly into a cold sink with no mat.

Acrylic

Acrylic products—sinks, tubs, and showers—are produced by a vacuum that pulls a solid sheet of acrylic into a mold. A high-quality acrylic sink is beautiful, quiet, and resists stains; and some models have germ-fighting properties built into the material. However, common acrylic is susceptible to surface scratches and cuts. Abrasive cleaning products will dull the surface, and metal pans can leave skid marks.

Karran USA, on the other hand, makes a high-density acrylic that is virtually indestructible, that no household chemical or food can stain, and whose color will not fade. Even bacteria and water cannot penetrate it. It is possible to use any household cleaner—even the toughest abrasives and bleach—without harming these sinks. The material is heat resistant to 400°F. You're looking at $200 and up.

Composite

Sinks made of a composite mix of stone, dust, and resin are quite popular. There are two types: shiny and dull. The shiny sinks emulate a porcelain-on-cast-iron finish (but are less heavy). The dull sinks emulate stone and may have a smooth or a semirough finish. The smooth finish can be scratched, but most scratches buff out easily. The semirough finish is advertised as heat, scratch, and stain resistant. Composite countertops often can be ordered with integral sinks. These sinks cost $200 and up.

Fireclay

Fireclay, also called vitreous china, is a high-end product. It is the same color all the way through and can have exquisite (even custom) detailing. If money is no object, this may be the sink for you; it's a work of art. Expect to pay $2,000 to $10,000 or more.

Handcrafted

Handcrafted copper sinks are another high-end option. One company, Oregon Copper Bowl, offers a variety of finishes: polished, satin coffee, antique patina, satin nickel, and stainless steel. For a double-bowl old farmhouse-style sink, expect to pay $3,000 to $4,000—and don't forget, you may need custom cabinetry to house it.

sink that is as scratch, stain, and chip resistant as possible. Each sink is mounted or installed in a certain way— for instance with a lip that hangs over the edge of the counter or is flush with the counter. See "Sink Mounting Options" on p. 104 for a discussion of these installations.

Two other factors to consider are bowl depth and shape. In this remodel, the bowls in the sink we are replacing are only 5 in. deep. The most common depth is 8 in., but dishwashing is easier with a depth of 9 in. or deeper. Generally, the deeper the bowl, the higher the price. A bowl that is rounded at the bottom corners is usually a lower-cost model. A square bowl is more spacious and will let stemware stand.

If you want more than two bowls, expect to pay a premium price. And keep in mind that multibowl sinks will normally be wide, as wide as 4 ft.; and that takes up a lot of counter space. You can also buy a stainless-steel sink with a built-in drain board, which is even wider.

Installation Considerations

THE SINK CUTOUT HOLE If you are replacing a sink and leaving the old countertop in place, keep in mind that you will not be able to opt for a smaller sink without replacing the countertop. The most common sink size is 33 in. by 22 in. from lip to lip, with the rough-in hole approximately 1 in. less in each direction, or 32 in. by 21 in. This may be the size hole you already have in your counter.

THE SINK'S DRAIN LOCATION A strainer positioned toward the rear of the bowl is preferable to the common center location because it keeps under-sink drain lines toward the back wall where

they will be out of the way. This type of drain also makes it easier to reach the strainer with your hand when the bowl is filled with plates.

Installing a Kitchen Sink

REPLACING BOTH COUNTER AND SINK Replacing a countertop is a matter of taking the existing measurements and passing them along to the supply store. Don't try to make any modifications to the top yourself. This is a job the manufacturer should do. Molded counters include corners as part of the complete unit. If you tell the manufacturer exactly where the sink will go in the countertop, it is likely they will cut the hole for a nominal fee or for free. Some molded sinks are one piece with the countertop.

Remove the old counter by first removing the sink and attached plumbing. Then look under the counter and remove any screws attaching the counter to the wall or cabinet. You may also need to cut through a bead of caulk before you can lift out the top.

When shopping for countertop material, find out the maximum length that is available, so you'll know whether your counter will have a seam. If it will, find out where the seam will be. If you will be installing a very long piece, ask out how many hands will be needed to install it so that it will not snap.

■ **WORK SAFE**
■ **WORK SMART**

If you are replacing both the sink and the counter, take a look at the latest selection of composite countertops with built-in sinks. These look neat, save installation labor, and don't leak. The drawback is that sink options are limited (for example, in material, bowl depth, and design).

Think before You Cut

Never cut the opening for, or build a counter around, a sink until you have the sink on site and you have verified that it is the right one. Otherwise, you may find out at the last minute that the sink is not available, the wrong model got shipped, the wrong color came in, it came in damaged, or you were given the wrong specs. Once you have possession of the sink, make sure its specs are as advertised. Keep it in its packing to protect it from damage.

Sink Mounting Options

Good: Self-Rimming Sink

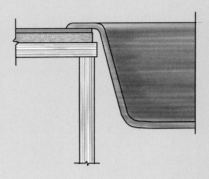

Better: Flush-Mount Sink

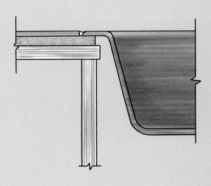

Best: Undermount Sink

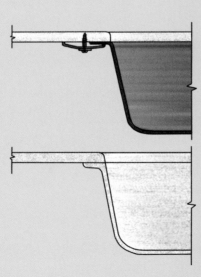

Sinks are attached to the countertop in three ways: on top of the counter (top mounted or "self-rimming"), level with the counter (flush mounted), and below the counter (undermounted). Some would also say that this order represents good, better, and best, but I think it is simply a matter of taste. The order does represent economical, expensive, and very expensive.

Top Mounted

Top-mounted sinks, commonly called self-rimming, are the popular choice because they are easy to install. If you have a laminate countertop, this is your only option. Simply cut a hole slightly smaller than the interior body of the sink, and drop it in. The outlying rim of the sink rests on top of the counter and supports the sink. A stainless-steel top-mounted sink is attached to the counter via special clips; a cast-iron sink is simply glued using silicone caulk.

Flush Mounted

Flush-mounted sinks sit level with the top of the counter and are best left for the pro to install. You can buy special sinks for this installation, or to save money and expand your options, you can sometimes use a common surface-mount sink. For instance, if you have a solid-surface counter, you can route out the counter's edge along the sink opening just deep enough so that the lip of the sink will sit flush with the counter. The same look can be achieved with an integrated sink—a countertop and sink unit that come in one piece.

I have also seen common top-mounted sinks installed flush by first attaching the sink to the plywood, then running backerboard up to the sink's rim, and finally laying tiles so they extend over part of the sink rim. However, the backerboard's edge will show unless you use find some type of special tile with a down-turned edge to cover it.

Undermount

Undermounted (or submounted) sinks have a neat, streamlined appearance since they have no lip that rises above the level of the countertop. There are different mounting methods, but basically the sink is clipped (and sometimes glued) in place from underneath. (This is like taking a common self-rimming sink but mounting it from underneath instead.) Many times you have to drill and tap the countertop, sometimes even putting in lead anchors. Extremely heavy sinks require independent support. The bottom line is: Installation should be left either to the pros in a fabrication shop or to the manufacturer.

Other Options

Custom sinks throw out the rules for the sake of artistic design. Such sinks can have designs both inside and out. For such a sink, as shown in the photo on p. 100, you would build a custom base to show it off to best advantage. For example, copper can be hand-beaten or finished in a variety of ways. One could even design in lights to highlight the design. Free-flow design concrete can make sinks that don't look like sinks.

If you are cutting a new sink hole, do it after the countertop has been installed so you can be sure to properly locate it, centered below a window, for example. To cut the hole and install the sink, follow the steps below, unless you have a custom sink such as granite. For this, you will have to bring in a specialist. For a tiled counter, cut the counter plywood and then wait for the tile installer to add the backerboard and tile. After that is done, you can install the sink.

STEP-BY-STEP SINK INSTALLATION

1. Verify that the new sink is the proper model, color, and size. Verify that it is not damaged.
2. Determine the location of the proposed sink on the countertop (which should already be installed). Typically it is centered under a window.
3. If your sink came with a template, trace around the template on the counter to form the cut line for the sink. If you do not have a template, follow steps 4 and 5.
4. Place the sink upside-down on the countertop where it is to be installed, being careful not to scratch the counter. As much as possible, center the sink on the counter front to back. Look under the counter and verify that you will not be cutting any counter bracing. If bracing is in the way, relocate the sink.
5. Trace around the sink with a pencil, lightly marking the counter. Remove the sink. Make another heavier mark ½ in. in from the first mark. This will be your cut line. Erase or cross out the outer line so you don't accidentally cut it.
6. It is common to use a 1½-in. hole cutter or sharp spade bit to drill the corners first, and then use a

WHAT CAN GO WRONG

You ruin the countertop by drilling the corner holes for the proposed sink dead center on the cut line, which places half the drilled hole outside the sink lip.

Sink and Faucet Replacement

Before: The homeowner wants this shallow, ugly sink to be replaced with something more attractive—of higher quality and with deeper bowls.

Disconnect the drains.

After the under-sink valves have been turned off, disconnect the water connections (turn counter-clockwise) to the faucet. Do not remove faucet hold-down nut; the faucet can stay on the sink.

Remove the sink hold-down screws.

After the sink has been pulled and the counter edge cleaned, place a bead of clear silicone around the sink hole.

After: Ugly sink out; beautiful sink and faucet in.

fine-tooth-blade jigsaw to cut the countertop. When you drill corners, do not make the mistake of putting the drill bit on the cut line. Only the outside of the cut arc should touch the line. Ask a helper to support the counter cutout piece as you cut the last few inches; otherwise, the blade may be pinched or the counter may crack as the cutout falls.

7. Install the strainers, as much of the drain as is practical, and the faucet before the sink is installed.

8. I normally put 100 percent clear silicone caulk around the perimeter of the cutout, to lock the sink in place once it is installed, and then slip the sink into the opening. Don't make the mistake I did as a youngster; watch your fingers.

REPLACING THE SINK IN THE OLD COUNTER By far the most common situation is to swap out the old sink for a new one of the same dimensions. And this is the real-life installation that I show in detail in this chapter.

Replacing a sink is easy enough, but you also need to disconnect and reconnect the supply and drain lines. Sometimes this will also mean relocating them. Often the trap pipes are located in the middle of the cabinet. If this is the case, I believe it is best to relocate the lines to the back or side of the cabinet so that the cabinet space will be more usable. In the example shown here, I had the option of moving the water lines to the right (I had no access underneath to relocate them to the back of the cabinet). In addition, I could not move the drain pipe at all because it came up through the cabinet bottom.

The following steps lead you through the job.

1. Verify that the new sink is the proper model, color, and size. Verify that it is not damaged.

2. Disconnect the under-sink drain lines (remember there is water in the trap).

3. Turn the stop valves off. Turn on the faucet and verify that the water pressure is gone.

4. Under the cabinet, position a bucket to catch the excess water, and disconnect the supply tubes from the faucets or from the stop valves (leave the faucet on the old sink).

5. For a stainless-steel or enamel-on-steel sink, loosen and remove all the sink hold-down clamps. For a cast-iron sink, slice through the caulk between the rim and the counter. A hair dryer can be used to soften the caulk to make it pull easier.

6. Pull out the sink, clean the countertop, and then add new caulk around the edge.

7. Attach the new faucet, strainers, and some of the drain/trap fittings to the strainer or wait until the sink is installed to attach it (a matter of personal preference).

8. Place the sink in the countertop cutout, and shoot in the attachment screws, if they're required by the manufacturer.

Pulling a Stuck Sink

If all goes well, the sink will pop out once the trap and any clips are disconnected. However, it may be glued to the countertop with silicone. If this is your situation, once the trap and any clips are disconnected, use a heat gun or a hair dryer to soften the silicone. Go around the sink lip slowly; it should take at least several minutes. The area should feel warm—almost hot. Then push up on the sink from underneath. If this doesn't work, slip a putty knife or a flat prybar (I grind the edge down until it is very thin) under the sink lip. Place a wedge or a piece of cardboard under the prybar to protect the countertop from scratches. Then pry up. The sink lip will still be warm.

Reconfiguring Under-Sink Drain Lines

Kitchen sink under-counter drains are ill-conceived. They drain slowly and often leak. This is because they use small-diameter trap pipe material with numerous compression joints (sometimes 10 or more), which seal via rubber and plastic gaskets that can leak after a few years (or the first time they are bumped). I've lost count of the number of rotted-out cabinet bottoms I've seen destroyed by this design. In addition, within some pipes, the effective water flow is reduced to a mere ½ in. at the horizontal to vertical turn. And the gasket located where the

Custom Drain System

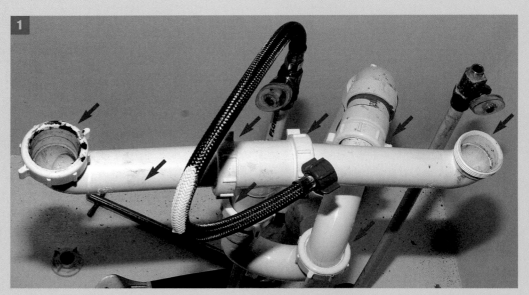

1. *Before:* Kitchen sink drains have many slip joints (*arrows*) that have a tendency to leak. Note that the water lines are in the center of the cabinet, rather than located along the back or side wall.

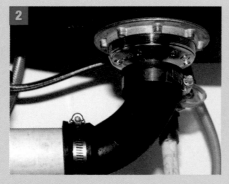

Once the old drain system has been removed, install flexible elbows onto each strainer and point 1½-in. schedule 40 PVC toward the rear wall.

If one strainer extends higher than the other, its connection can be lowered via a 1½-in. cleanout (screwed onto the strainer threads). The flexible elbow slips onto the cleanout hub.

drain pipe attaches to the strainer threads may further reduce the drain opening.

Frustrated with the common under-sink drain system, I normally install my own custom-designed system, which gets all the under-sink piping out of the way and mounts it securely against the back wall so it cannot budge if bumped. To

make it more heavy duty, the drain pipes are built of schedule 40, 1½-in. pipe (typical under-sink, thin-wall drain pipes are a little over 1 in. inside diameter), so the two sink bowls drain faster and the pipes never clog. Beneath the bowl, a full opening at the strainer output also aids the fast draining of the bowl. The biggest

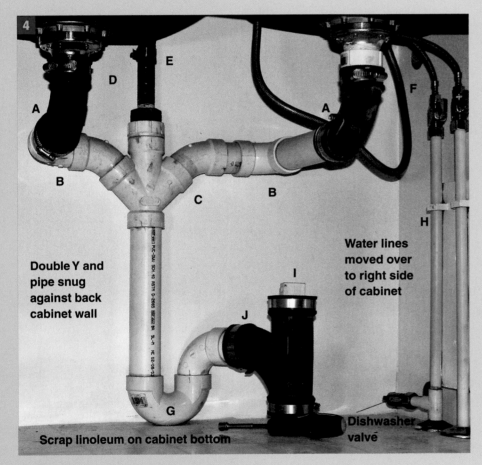
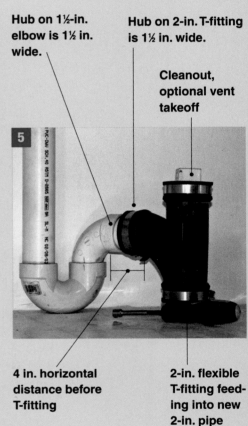

4. *After:* This custom design drain system drains fast and does not leak. *A,* flexible elbows; *B,* PVC elbow; *C,* double Y-fitting; *D,* dishwasher connection (PVC cleanout fitting glued into top of Y-fitting; 1½-in. by ¾-in. galvanized reducing bushing screwed into PVC cleanout; ¾-in. galvanized nipple screwed into bushing); *E,* behind-sink dishwasher hose (slips over galvanized pipe, fastened via marine clamp); *F,* 1½-in. PVC cleanout fitting (screwed onto strainer threads of shallow bowl to equalize differing bowl depths); *G,* trap; *H,* flexible 2-in. T-fitting; *I,* optional vent tie-in location; *J,* horizontal distance to T-fitting (4 in.).

Kitchen Sink Drain Lines

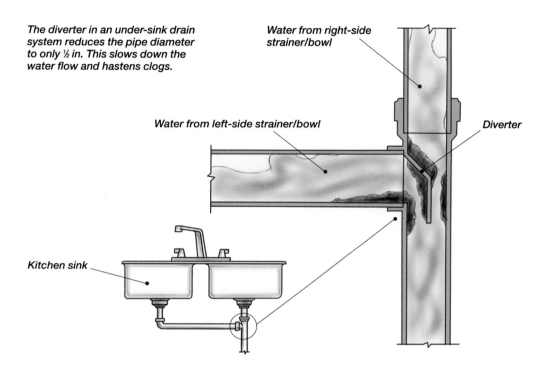

The diverter in an under-sink drain system reduces the pipe diameter to only ½ in. This slows down the water flow and hastens clogs.

Water from right-side strainer/bowl

Water from left-side strainer/bowl

Diverter

Kitchen sink

bonus of using my system is that the glued or clamped fittings are less likely to leak than the usual compression fittings with gaskets, especially when bumped. I have installed this system in commercial installations where the pipes get smashed every day by workers kicking the mop bucket under sink, and it has yet to leak.

INSTALLING THE STRAINERS

1. My design starts with Kohler 8801 heavy-duty strainers, which are in my opinion the best strainers on the market. Their only disadvantage is cost: about $40 each. They are made of solid brass (they are heavy), and have cut threads on the bottom where the drain line attaches to the strainer. Most other strainers use shallow rolled threads; often with

these, the plastic nut pops off as you attempt to tighten it to stop a leak.

2. I attach the strainers to the sink with clear 100 percent silicone caulk. The caulk acts as a glue securely fastening the strainer to the bowl. With this method, the large under-sink nut that holds the strainer tight against the bowl could completely come loose and the strainer would not leak between the bowl and strainer lip. I do not recommend plumber's putty because it tends to harden, crack, and leak.

CHOOSING DRAIN PIPE AND FITTINGS

For the under-sink drain I use 1½-in., schedule 40 drain pipe. For fittings, I use both rigid (which are glued) and flexible types. Flexible PVC fittings, originally

Installing Heavy-Duty Strainers

Before: The customer wants the ugly, leaky strainer replaced. The pipe-to-strainer gasket (*arrow*) cuts off the diameter of the drain by 50 percent.

Apply clear silicone to the lip of the strainer or sink strainer hole, and squish the strainer into place in the bowl. Be sure to center it.

From under the sink, place the rubber gasket and cardboard ring against the sink bottom (both under the large brass nut), and then tighten. Needle-nose pliers (nose wrapped with electrical tape) are inserted through the strainer slots to keep the unit from turning.

After: Ugly strainer out; beautiful strainer in. Also note that there are no gasket obstructions (*arrow*) to slow the flow of water.

known as Fernco fittings, look, feel, and smell like rubber. They are sold at most plumbing and hardware stores. They slip over the pipe and fasten with stainless clamps. Since they disconnect quickly and easily, they can be used as cleanout fittings when pipes need to be augered or snaked. The old under-floor drain line to the sink will be changed from 1½ in. to 2 in.

ATTACHING PIPE WHEN BOWLS ARE THE SAME DEPTH For each sink bowl, I attach a flexible elbow onto each strainer thread and point it toward the back wall. From there I install rigid PVC pipe to the back wall and glue on a rigid elbow and a short piece of pipe to point toward the center of the sink. Both of these pipes glue into a double-Y with a center piece coming off for the optional dishwasher connection. Out of its bottom comes a short piece of pipe that dumps into a schedule 40 P-trap. The P-trap feeds into the drain line coming out of the wall or floor.

In this situation, the pipe between the P-trap and the flexible T is 3 in. long. It looks shorter since part of its length is hidden in the hubs of the fittings. Thus the angle of the photo may make the system look like a glorified S-trap, it is not because I followed the 2x rule, by which the minimum distance (from trap to pipe turn down) needs to be at least twice the diameter of the pipe (here, 1½ in.). It reality, I have made this distance even longer because the measuring distance starts at the trap weir (water), which is still farther along.

In the real-life case illustrated here, the distance between the trap weir and the point where the fitting turns is about 4 in. If needed, all pipe is secured against the back wall with metal strapping.

ATTACHING PIPE WHEN BOWLS ARE DIFFERENT DEPTHS When a sink has bowls of different depths, it is difficult to get all the pipes to align on the back wall. To solve this problem, I extend the under-sink fitting of the shallower bowl to the depth of the deep bowl's via a schedule 40 cleanout fitting (discard the plug). One end of the fitting has 1½-in. female threads, and the opposite end is 1½-in. pipe. The fitting screws onto the threads of the strainer (apply thread sealant), and its opposite end slips into the hub of a flexible 90, which, in turn, points toward the back wall.

MOVING THE WATER LINES At the same time I reconfigured the drain lines, I also moved the water lines to the right side of the cabinet (see photo 4 on p. 109), positioning them 1½ in. from the cabinet wall. This way, I could still put the escutcheon (flange) around the pipe and mount a 2x6 on the cabinet wall to attach the pipes to. (My first choice is always to secure pipes along the rear of the cabinet adjacent to the drain line; but in this case, I didn't have access to that area in the basement.)

VENTING As always, venting can be a hassle. In this real-life situation, there was no existing vent for the kitchen. To increase air circulation, there are three options: increasing the drain diameter to 2 in., adding an AAV, or taking an individual vent off the top of my new 2-in. T and ripping out the walls and roof to install it. The latter option is way too expensive. The AAV option is fine, and I may use it later. But since I dislike 1½-in. kitchen lines, I decided to change the line over to 2 in. The increased diameter will allow the air within the pipes to freely move over the water so no siphoning will take place. (There is a 3-in. vent in the line where the 2-in. line ties into the main 3-in line.) Though this venting method (increasing the drain pipe diameter) works well, it is not allowed in all areas. Check with your inspector about his or her venting preferences.

PROTECTING THE CABINET FLOOR
The last thing I do is put a scrap piece of linoleum on the bottom of the cabinet. It sort of gives the place a little class and at the same time keeps all the water off the wood.

Installing a Dishwasher in an Existing Cabinet

Installing a dishwasher is easy if you are remodeling the entire kitchen: simply leave a 24-in.-wide space between cabinets where you want the dishwasher. Installing in existing cabinetry is more time-consuming because in addition to electrical and plumbing work, you need to cut into the cabinetry to create space for the dishwasher. And as luck would have it, in our real-life situation shown here, this is what I do.

Is There Room?

The first step is deciding where to install the dishwasher and verifying that there is enough room (left to right in the existing cabinet). Dishwashers are normally installed adjacent to the sink, most often on the right side since most people are right-handed. Left-handed people may prefer the dishwasher to the left of the sink. Whichever side you choose, be sure the kitchen door or oven door will not hit the dishwasher door when it's open.

To verify that there is enough room horizontally, take some measurements. A standard full-size dishwasher needs a 24-in. horizontal rough-in cutout to fit snugly into the cabinet. If 24 in. takes you into an adjacent cabinet in addition to the one next to the sink or cuts into the support structure of the sink, you will have to opt for a space-saver unit as I did here. Space savers need only an 18-in. hole. A full-size unit is usually the first choice, but small is better than nothing.

If budget permits you can rework the entire cabinet system. However, in the project shown here the existing cabinets were custom-built on site, and the owner did not want them reworked. Make no cuts in the cabinets until the dishwasher

Where the cabinet opening is 18 in. wide, the customer may opt for a space-saver dishwasher rather than lose adjoining cabinetry.

Typical Dishwasher

Once the dishwasher is out of the box, remove the bottom kick plate to expose the electrical and plumbing hookups.

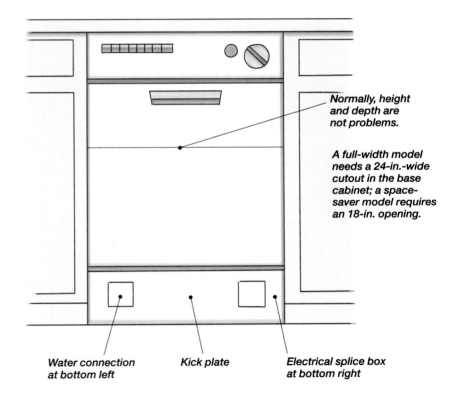

Normally, height and depth are not problems.

A full-width model needs a 24-in.-wide cutout in the base cabinet; a space-saver model requires an 18-in. opening.

Water connection at bottom left — *Kick plate* — *Electrical splice box at bottom right*

Adding a Dishwasher

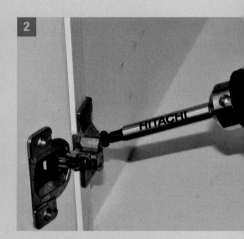

The first step is to remove the cabinet door. Use a cordless drill and a long Phillips-head driver.

Before: A standard 24-in.-wide dishwasher will not fit into these cabinets without destroying the adjoining cabinets.

Next, remove the cabinet hardware, which is usually attached with Phillips-head screws.

With a black marker, draw the lines where the cabinet has to be cut to allow the dishwasher to slide in.

Using a reciprocating saw with a long, fine-tooth blade, cut 2 in. to 3 in. along the line from the cabinet front.

Use a jigsaw to cut the cabinet shelf. Cut the last 2 in. to 3 in. with a reciprocating saw (not shown).

Pull in the power cable for the dishwasher and loop it along the back wall. Here a long-abandoned plumbing hole to the basement was available in the back wall.

Remove additional insulation from the dishwasher wire—to double (*left*) the stripping length supplied by the manufacturer (*right*).

Install the NM connector in the electrical box wire entrance hole. Splice the power cable to the dishwasher wires (black to black, white to white, bare wire to green grounding screw), then reinstall the cover plate.

Using a spade bit, drill a hole in the panel (upper back) adjacent to the sink for the dishwasher drain line, then one close to the bottom for the water line.

Tilting the dishwasher on its side, attach a ⅜-in. male thread by ⅜-in. outer diameter (supply tube size) angle fitting in the plumbing inlet hole. When finished tightening, point the fitting toward the back wall.

Attach one end of the dishwasher supply pipe to the water inlet fitting just installed.

You're ready to slide the dishwasher in. The drain is at the upper left and the water line at the bottom left. The power cable is taped out of the way on the back wall.

After: The dishwasher has been slid into place and secured. Only one cabinet section had to be removed.

Replacing an Old Dishwasher

If you are replacing a dishwasher, first shut off the circuit breaker and test to verify that the power is off. Remove the kickplate of the existing dishwasher to verify that the unit will slide out. Sometimes you will find that additional flooring (tile, stone, etc.) or subflooring was installed in front of the dishwasher so that you can't slide out the old or slide in the new without cutting the floor—and most people don't want their floor damaged. To reduce the height of the old dishwasher, you can screw its feet up into the frame using a small adjustable wrench and pliers. But remember, you must do this to the two back feet as well. To get the lowest height on a new dishwasher, remove all four feet.

Sometimes an old dishwasher will slide right out with plumbing and wiring still attached. Other times the plumbing and wiring keep it fastened in place. For these units, you will have to disconnect everything before the unit will slide out. Remember to remove the electrical power and shut off the water. The drain line is normally a flexible pipe and will slide out with the washer once it is disconnected from under the kitchen sink.

is on site, and you have verified it is the right model, color, etc.

Vertical room for a dishwasher is rarely a problem. Kitchen sink counters are normally installed at a height of approximately 35 in. from the finished floor to the underside of the countertop. A dishwasher needs 34½ in. to 35 in., and its legs can adjust up another inch if needed. If your cabinets are extra high, you can install a trim piece over the unit.

Once I have the dishwasher on site and have verified that it is the right unit, I remove the cabinet door and hardware. Then I mark the cabinet where I want to cut it.

My primary cutting tool is the jigsaw, which cuts everything but the area up against a wall. (Its base plate gets in the way, but I do have the option of removing the base plate.) To cut closer, I normally use my reciprocating saw. With both saws, I use metal-cutting blades to make a slow, fine cut. The cut will remove all of the cabinet's shelves, the upper bracing on the cabinet facing the front, and the trim.

Electrical

The dishwasher needs a 20-amp circuit breaker all to itself. Normally, I bring the 12-2 NMB cable up through the floor along the very back wall and make a large loop, then feed it under to the splice box on the dishwasher's front right. (For instructions on running cable and installing a new circuit breaker, see my book *Wiring a House,* Taunton Press, 2002.) The large loop makes it easy to pull out the dishwasher for maintenance or repairs. I do the same with the dishwasher's drain and water lines. The dishwasher's splice box will have a hole for the incoming cable; be sure to install an NM clamp first and then take the cable through it. The clamp is to be tightened onto cable only to snug; never super tight. Within the splice box, connect the black wire of the cable to the black wire of the dishwasher. Do the same with the white wires. Connect the cable ground wire to the frame or to the green dishwasher wire.

Drain Line

Never cut the drain hose that comes attached to the dishwasher. Use it all. As the drain line exits the dishwasher, it should loop up high (just under the counter via a hole in the cabinet), arc down to the kitchen drain line, and then tie into the drain just before the sink's trap. Never add a trap just for the dishwasher.

Local codes may require that an air gap device be installed. Most national codes no longer require this and neither do most manufacturers. An air gap device is an ugly item that attaches to the sink, normally in the sprayer hole. (If you want a sprayer, you may have to punch or drill a second hole in the sink.) The device has two pipes sticking out below the sink. One pipe is for the dishwasher drain and the other goes to the sink drain. If you have a garbage disposal, there will be a knockout available for the dishwasher drain. If your sink has no garbage disposal but has the common white, thin-wall polypropylene trap pipes, you can attach the dishwasher drain with an extension pipe—called a dishwasher tailpiece—that has a side inlet for the disposal.

Rather than work with the standard leaky drain system found under most sinks, I usually rip out everything and install my own design using schedule 40 pipe (see "Reconfiguring Under-Sink Drain Lines" on p. 108). This allows me to connect the dishwasher drain into a ¾-in. pipe.

Water Line

The drain hose comes already attached to the washer, but not so the water line. The easiest hookup method is to buy a pre-made ⅜-in. dishwasher line with the end fittings already on. The washer normally comes with a female ⅜-in. threaded connection pointing straight to the floor. Since there is rarely enough room to make a turn with the pipe, I install an angle fitting (⅜-in. male thread by ⅜-in. outer diameter compression) into the dishwasher. This allows the incoming pipe to attach to the washer parallel to the floor. To attach to the hot-water line under the kitchen sink, I normally do one of two things: replace the existing fixture shutoff valve (hot-water side) with one that has two outlets (one for the kitchen faucet and one for the dish-

washer) or cut a T into the line and add a fixture shutoff valve there.

Finishing Up

Once the electrical and plumbing lines have been attached, you're ready to slide the dishwasher into its space to finish the job. Do this carefully so the sides of the dishwasher aren't damaged. Once in, adjust the legs so the top of the dishwasher cabinet is close to the underside of the counter and shoot the dishwasher frame attachment screws (the two brackets on the front top of the tub) into the counter. If this is not done, the dishwasher could tilt forward as the door is opened. Job done. Add trim if wanted.

Getting the Bad Taste Out of Your Ice

Ice-maker ice sometimes has a bad taste due to iron in the water. If the water tastes bad out of the faucet, it will taste bad out of the ice maker. To correct this, either buy a fridge with a built-in carbon filter or add one by cutting into the ice-maker water line. The first option obviously is easier. When shopping for a fridge, look for one with a large carbon filter that is easily accessible for changing. If you must install an in-line carbon filter, it can be installed anywhere in the ice-maker line (usually behind the fridge). It will normally be cigar-shaped with compression fittings on each side (¼ in. outer diameter).

Copper in the water lends a metallic after-taste to ice and fridge water. The culprit is not the pipe so much as it is the aggressive water eating away at the pipe. If you run the sink faucet for a minute or two you can rid the sink water of the taste. But this does not work for water in the ice-maker line. One solution is to treat the house water with an acid neutralizer.

Plumbing water to a new, modern fridge can get you ice water, cubed ice, and crushed ice—all without opening the door. Once you have it, you never want to be without.

ACCORDING TO CODE

Do not use clear tubing for the water line since it is rarely made from approved water line material.

■ **WORK**

Cover the tubing's cut end with electrical tape until you are ready to use it. This keeps debris from falling in as the tubing is pushed and pulled.

WHAT CAN GO WRONG

You tap the dishwasher line into the cold-water line rather than the hot-water line.

Plumbing in an Ice-Maker Line

Ice makers in refrigerators, once a luxury item, have become almost a necessity. Once you have become accustomed to easy access to cold water, cubed ice, and crushed ice, it's hard to go back. An ice-maker line is small-diameter (¼-in. outer diameter) tubing. Most likely, you will be tapping it into a ½-in. cold-water line a distance away.

Finding Access

To run tubing for the ice maker, you will need access. Under-floor access is easiest if it's available. If not, open the walls to run ½-in. pipe from the tapping-in location to behind the fridge.

If you come through the back wall behind the fridge, you can install a small box in the wall to hide the valve where the pipe terminates. The tubing to the refrigerator will come off the valve inside that box.

Running Tubing

To run ¼-in. outer diameter tubing, drill a ⅜-in. hole behind the fridge next to the trim. Pull enough tubing through from underneath to make one or two circular loops about 2 ft. in diameter behind the fridge. The loops give you some breathing room when the appliance needs to be moved for maintenance or repairs. The best pipe to use is the metal-braided or white flexible pipe with premade ends; be sure to drill the hole large enough for the end-fitting to get through.

I do not recommend running copper tubing. It kinks easily and also gets eaten through quickly by aggressive water. Its wall thickness is proportional to its outer diameter; thus small pipe has very thin walls. I have had ¼-in.-diameter copper (in my own house) spring pinholes (and flood the kitchen) within 6 months after installation. And this was with neutral (pH 7) spring water. I had to change it all out to nonmetallic.

Tapping In

A saddle valve is the most common way of tapping an ice-maker line into a water line. It bolts around the pipe. The saddle valve has a sharp, pointed hollow needle that will puncture the pipe. Be sure to read the instructions to verify that you will puncture the right place. Galvanized pipe will have to be drilled (read the manufacturer's instructions for hole size). Do not use a saddle valve on supply tube-size pipe (⅜ in. outer diameter) because the pipe is too small. Check the back of the fridge to see if there is a clamp for an ice-maker pipe to run through just before it attaches to the fridge. Not using the

The two most common water line to fridge attachment points.

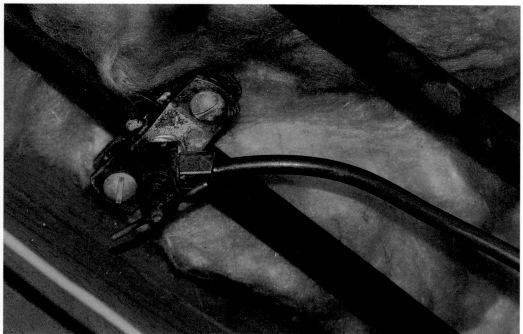

Saddle valves tap into a water line by punching a tiny hole. Some valves and some pipes require you to predrill a hole in the pipe.

WORK SAFE
WORK SMART

When drilling a round surface such as galvanized pipe, first "ding" the pipe with a nail set and hammer. This will create a small concave surface to set the drill bit in.

WHAT CAN GO WRONG

You tap the ice-maker line into the hot-water line rather than the cold-water line.

WHAT CAN GO WRONG

You angle the tubing as it enters the compression fitting. This almost guarantees a leak.

clamp may cause a leak at the compression fitting.

If you don't use a saddle valve, cut into the main water line, and insert a T-fitting. Add a short length of pipe, a male adapter, and then a fixture shutoff valve (½-in. female thread by ¼-in. outer diameter compression).

Working with Different Pipe

When working with CPVC, don't make the mistake of using a plastic male adapter to screw into the fixture shutoff's female thread. The plastic threads sometimes don't go deep enough, or they may crack; in either event, leakage will result.

If you use copper tubing for the ice-maker line, double-check the compression connection an hour or two later to be sure there is no leak.

If you use PEX, you will have to tee off a main line and then dead end into what is called a drain fitting (a crimp on one end and ¼-in. outer diameter male on the other) or use the manufacturer's special ice-maker T-and-valve assembly. Don't cut into the lines unless you have a PEX crimper or other proprietary tool. If none is available, use a compression T.

Finishing Touches

Now you're ready for the last steps. First, make sure the fridge is plugged in. Then turn on the valve releasing water to the appliance, and check for leaks. Finally, be sure to caulk the hole behind the fridge with a fire-stop-type caulk.

Don't expect ice for a day or two because it takes time for the air in the lines (within the fridge) to be replaced by water.

PEX valves for ice-maker lines. The bottom one, made by Vanguard, cuts directly into a PEX line, while the smaller valve installs at the end of a line.

Premade Ice-Maker Water Lines

Premade ice-maker water lines are more expensive than running copper tubing pipe, but they have so many advantages, I recommend them. Copper tubing (¼ in. outer diameter) costs about $20 per 50-ft. roll; premade lines cost twice that. Premade nonmetallic ice-maker water lines typically come in 10-ft. lengths, but lengths up to 20 ft. are also available. The premade lines save you:

- The challenge of installing thin copper without kinking.

- The difficulty of creating compression ends that won't leak.

- The worry about active water eating away at the copper over time.

■ **WORK**

Do not plumb the fridge ice-maker water line in areas that might freeze such as an exterior wall, attic, or crawlspace. Such lines are small in diameter and will freeze rapidly.

■ **WORK**

For premade ice-maker water lines, the diameter of the drilled hole in the floor behind the fridge (and all other holes) has to exceed the diameter of the compression nut on the pipe end, not just the pipe.

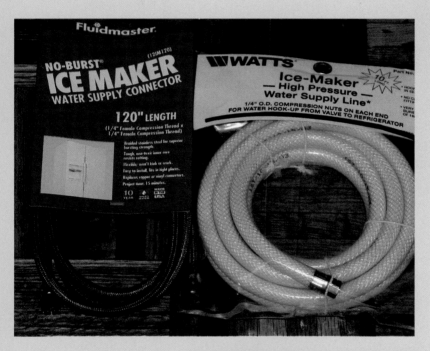

Premade ice-maker water lines install faster and eliminate the need to create compression ends, which occasionally leak.

Are Disposals and Septic Systems Compatible?

I am often asked, "Is there a problem using a disposal if I have a septic tank?" The answer is no. Go right ahead and install one. You should not have problems with a disposal unless your basic kitchen plumbing has serious problems that a disposal might worsen, such as existing drain lines of steel or cast iron that are half-closed, a deep sag in the disposal pipe over a long run, or an uphill run. For those who are skeptical (despite my reassurances) that a garbage disposal will work with their septic system, In-Sink-Erator makes a special disposal for houses with septic tanks. It injects a liquid biotreatment into the grinding chamber that contains millions of active microorganisms to digest food waste before it even reaches the septic tank.

This biotreatment disposal by In-Sink-Erator, is perfect for houses with septic tanks.

Adding a Garbage Disposal

Many people like to have a disposal in the kitchen sink. If you plan to install a disposal, think about the many options available before you make your purchase.

Power

For light-duty loads you can get by with a ⅓-hp or ½-hp (horsepower) unit. If you do a lot of cooking/cleaning and will be using the disposal every day or even several times a day, opt for a ¾-hp or 1-hp unit.

Noise

Higher-priced units are quieter because the design includes sound suppression,

If you are tired of removing food scraps from the kitchen strainer, you need to install a disposal, such as the unit on the left.

most often via a baffle around the grinding chamber, which is where most of the noise comes from. In-Sink-Erator advertises a double baffle. Another noise suppression option is a removable sound plug to cover the grinder opening. The plug does significantly reduce noise, but it is easy to lose. Noise, through vibration, is also transmitted to the sink. The noisiest sinks will be the low-cost thin stainless-steel sinks that do not come with built-in soundproofing (see "Picking a Stainless-Steel Sink" on p. 101). Even if you have a high-end sink, choose a disposal that includes a rubber damper between the sink and the disposal.

Wiring

You cannot tie into the kitchen receptacle circuit. You need to run a new circuit (12-2 NMB with ground). You can hard wire the disposal or take it, via cord and plug, to a receptacle under the counter. It does not need to be GFCI protected. If

you have a small disposal (⅓ hp to ½ hp), codes may allow you to tie it to the kitchen light circuit, but this is not recommended. (For wiring instructions, see my book *Wiring a House*.)

Switch

People tend to forget about the little detail of the switch. The installation of the switch, however, can cost more than the disposal itself. A wall switch may be the first choice, but there are other less-complicated options:

- *Batch feed disposal:* You fill the disposal with whatever, close the lid at the strainer (and then back it out a quarter turn) and the unit turns on. Run the water.
- *Common continuous-feed disposal:* This is controlled by a switch that is typically mounted on the wall behind the sink. However, to minimize costs, it can also be mounted

Garbage Disposal Installation

Disposal bottom. *A,* hole for the NM connector that holds the cord or cable; *B,* electrical splice is under this lid (remove to wire, then replace; go ahead and wire plug and cord into the disposal before you install it: black to black, white to white, and green to ground screw); *C,* red button overload switch (press this switch if unit does not work); *D,* unjam screw (insert hex-head wrench supplied with disposal and turn to unjam unit; be sure unit is off).

Before: An under-sink drain system with no disposal.

Start by removing the drain pipes and sink strainer. *Note*: This strainer had no plumber's putty under it; but, amazingly enough, it was not leaking.

Remove the attachment flange from the disposal (it just lifts off), and pop loose the split ring to pull the assembly apart.

Insert the hub from above (use 100 percent silicone rather than plumber's putty), and slip the disposal attachment flange onto the hub from underneath while pressing hub down from above. Popping the split ring back on the hub will hold all parts onto the hub.

Using an electrician's speed screwdriver, spin the three flange nuts up, to tighten the unit onto the sink.

With one hand (unseen), lift the disposal directly under the strainer hole while the opposite hand turns the disposal attachment mating flange. The disposal will attach immediately with no hassle. The unit is now attached to the sink.

continued . . .

Garbage Disposal Installation *continued*

After cutting a flat-ended drain pipe to length (to reach from the disposal output to the sink drain T), insert the rubber gasket (supplied with the disposal) over the pipe's flat circular end.

Attach the pipe to the disposal, via the bolt supplied with the unit, and to the drain sink T.

Attach the dishwasher hose (pipe at upper right) to the disposal inlet (remove the internal knockout first).

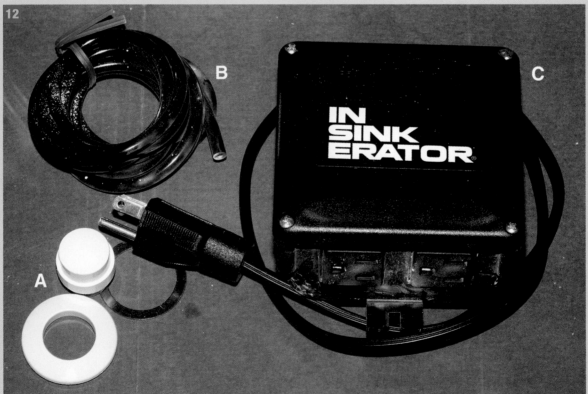

An air switch eliminates the need for wiring in an electrical switch to turn the disposal on. *A,* the push button will install on the sink top; *B,* the air hose connects from push button to the black module; *C,* the black module mounts under the sink. (Plug the disposal into it; plug the module into an unswitched receptacle.)

under the sink right behind the cabinet door.

■ *Special sink-top switch made by the manufacturer:* This is a nonelectrical push-button air switch that mounts right on the sink itself. A little hollow air tube goes from the switch to a power module box under the sink. The module plugs into an always-on receptacle outlet. The disposal, in turn, plugs into the module.

Plumbing

The plumbing for a disposal is normally a simple affair. Remove the sink strainer, install the disposal support ring, and then mount the disposal onto the ring. The hard part, if any, is plumbing the output of the disposal into the existing sink drain. This should be done before the sink trap. Do not plumb in a separate trap for the disposal. The second sink bowl and the disposal should share a trap.

Uneven bowls sometimes pose a problem. Always try to mount the disposal on the highest bowl. You can mount the disposal on the low bowl only if the disposal's drain can make it to the trap without going uphill.

Running a dishwasher drain into a disposal is simplicity itself. Every disposal comes with a pipe sticking out of its upper side, which is meant to attach to the dishwasher drain hose. Inside this pipe is a thin plastic knockout that has to be punched out if a dishwasher is being added. Simply insert a screwdriver into the disposal pipe opening and hit it with a hammer. You will feel the knockout break away. There are no plumbing pipes to install. The only problem you might have is if the dishwasher drain hose and the disposal input pipe are two different diameters. For this use a coupling device (available at all plumbing supply houses), which can serve as an adapter to join the two different diameters.

Operating Tips

If the unit jams, many of the upper-end units will instantly reverse direction. Jamming happens when you add waste to a continuous-feed unit (and turn it on) before you start running the water. If the unit stays jammed, first verify that the switch is turned off. Then insert a hex-head wrench (which comes with the disposal and is normally ¼ in.) into the hex-head hole in the unit bottom, and turn to break it free.

Here's some more good advice:

■ To get rid of the foul smell from the disposal, cut up a lemon and grind it in the disposal (you can also add baking soda).

■ Stringy-type items like corn husks do not grind well and can "string up" all the little cutters inside.

■ Do not pour hot grease into the disposal because as it solidifies as it cools.

■ If the disposal ever fails to work, there is normally a red reset button on the disposal bottom.

■ If a ring falls into the disposal, turn the unit off as fast as you can. The ring may be saved if you act fast enough. If you do not find the ring in the disposal itself, look in the sink trap. If not there, and if you acted quickly, it's in the lines. Use no water in the house. You will have to cut all the lines apart (and perhaps the walls) in the attempt to find it. Otherwise, it is long gone. The chance of finding a ring in a septic tank is almost zero.

■ This should be obvious: Never put your hand into a running disposal. To be really safe, tape the switch in the off position before you put your hand in, especially if there is a second person in the kitchen.

CHAPTER 5

Bathroom Remodeling

WHILE THE KITCHEN has evolved into a sociable hub, the bathroom has become more of a comfortable retreat, a private place to relax and unwind. Fixtures and furnishings help set the tone for the room. When they are more than just functional—adding a special style or appeal—they make the bathroom more pleasant and inviting.

As you remodel or add on to your bathroom, expect the unexpected. Many older bath/shower units were designed with no thought for future maintenance. In addition, if the home is older, the walls may not be plumb or square and the joists may not be level. The remodel projects featured in this chapter will show you how to overcome these problems.

Boring to Unique Showerheads

Showers can be boring—or showers can be fun and relaxing. I prefer the latter. And so do many others as indicated by

Once you install this Zoe dual-pan shower-head, you'll never go back to the boring and ordinary again.

Drop-ear elbows (sometimes called winged elbows).

Beware all-plastic drop-ear elbows. They have a tendency to leak and crack.

the upward sales of specialty showerheads. Replacing a showerhead is an easy job that delivers a huge return; it is often the first remodel work done in a home. Showerhead designs offer water that cascades, rains, or pulsates from the fixture. Multihead fixtures offer a spray of water from more than one location within the shower.

Though the work of upgrading a showerhead may be easy, look before you leap. First, take a look at the shower arm, which is the chrome pipe that connects to the showerhead. Is it anchored securely to the wall? Grab the shower-

head and see if the arm moves around. If it does, you will need to secure it inside the wall using a plumbing fitting called a drop-ear elbow. The fitting mounts to a nailer (also called *blocking*) placed flat between two studs inside the shower wall immediately behind where the shower arm goes into the wall. The drop-ear elbow fitting has female threads for the arm at one end, and its right-angle end points down to connect to the pipe coming out of the shower faucet mounted below. I normally attach the fitting to the nailer via two drywall screws.

It is possible that a drop-ear elbow was used (even though the pipe flops around), and that whatever it was attached to was not secured. Either way, you will need to rip open the wall immediately behind the showerhead. If you are lucky, there will be a closet behind, and you need only remove a piece of paneling. If not, you may have to rip out finished walls, which can be quite expensive. Since the work is done from behind, you do not need to rip out the finished plumbing wall in the bath. However, if your home has two showers back to back, one wall will have to be cut into.

Next, decide whether the shower arm will stay or go. A chrome arm is inexpensive to replace, but if it must be kept, you'll want to remove the old showerhead with minimal scratching to the pipe. Since a common pipe wrench or pair of pliers has teeth that will cut into the arm's fancy finish, we must find a way around that problem.

Here's the most common and easiest way to remove a showerhead pipe: First remove the showerhead, next insert the handle of a pair of slip-joint pliers into the pipe end, and then turn counterclockwise. A strap wrench can be used, but the strap will have to be roughed up with plumber's cloth to keep it from slipping.

Sometimes nothing less than a pipe wrench will work. If possible, loosen the pipe from inside the wall cavity, so the scratches won't be seen. As a last resort, wrap electrical tape (or a rag) around the pipe and use a pipe wrench outside the wall cavity. This method minimizes but does not always eliminate scratches.

Multiple Showerheads

If you want to shower with your spouse or relax your aching body in a multiple spray of soothing warmth, a shower equipped with two or more showerheads may be for you. Women especially love multiple showerheads because the extra water rinses hair faster and makes it easier to shave legs. (Don't ask me how; this is what my wife tells me.)

For best results, the shower stall should be spacious: 5 ft., the length of a common tub, is the minimum length for a shower holding two people. Contrary to what you might think, a standard tub is not too narrow. My wife prefers to have the heads vertical as opposed to horizontal, and she only uses two of our three heads. Actually, a three-head unit is a bit of overkill. A two-head unit works best in a common tub or shower stall. If space is tight, consider a neo (corner-style) shower that is 38 in. by 38 in., but don't expect it to hold two people.

SHOWERHEADS INSTALLED IN A SINGLE LOCATION You can make your own home-grown multiple-showerhead system by simply adding a T to the pipe (inside the wall or out) that runs from the faucet body to the showerhead or even in the shower arm itself; I have done so many times. However, the easiest (and by far the nicest looking) way to upgrade to a multiple-showerhead system is to simply remove the old showerhead and angled chrome pipe and screw in a purchased unit. A number of good-looking options

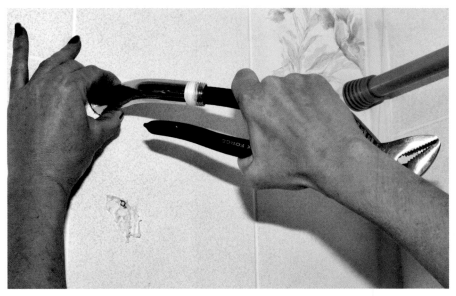

The best way to tighten or loosen a shower pipe is to insert an insulated handle of adjustable pliers within the pipe and then turn.

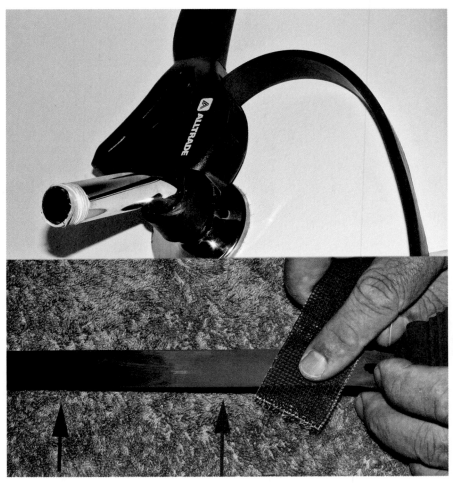

A strap wrench will not scratch the finish on a pipe but has a tendency to slip. To minimize slipping, rough up the strap with some plumber's cloth.

are available, but the units made by Zoe (888-287-1757 www.showerbuddy.com) are the ones I install most often.

SHOWERHEADS INSTALLED IN DUAL LOCATIONS The problem with having a shower partner is that one person gets the water and the other freezes—not very romantic, or even practical. Multiple-head units installed in a single location help somewhat in getting the spray to the back of the stall. But it's much nicer if each showering party has his or her own spray and temperature control. You can do this simply by running two heads off of one valve body. Pipe to the second head can be either exposed (low-class, but economical) or hidden in the wall. I got a couple married by doing this. My customer (a college professor) mentioned he was going to propose to his girlfriend that evening. So I installed two shower-heads (one on each side of the shower) and told him to propose to her in the shower. They are now married and living happily ever after.

If is much better however, to have two valves—one valve for each shower-head—so you can control both water volume and temperature. This installa-tion is much easier with new construc-tion; otherwise, you'll need to rip open walls to get at the pipe and faucet.

Getting More Hot Water

The trouble with multiple heads is that you run out of hot water a lot faster. So be sure to choose a unit that has a separate valve at each showerhead so you can shut off or lower the water volume to head(s) not being used, to maximize your hot-water time. You can also increase your hot-water tank's capacity by installing a second water heater in series with the existing heater (discussed in Chapter 6).

This Zoe multiple showerhead assembly is horizontal. However, many prefer to install a two-head system and turn the unit vertical.

Choosing a Shower Faucet

As you shop for a shower faucet, look for one that controls water volume as well as temperature. Other desirable features include the ability to self-adjust for varying water pressure (via pressure-balancing valves) and antiscald protection. The latter two features are required by code in most areas, and I won't install a shower faucet without them.

Converting a Tub-Only Faucet to a Tub/Shower

If you have a two-handle, bath-only faucet that you'd like to upgrade to a tub/shower, your plumbing work will probably be easy. The existing faucet con-trol likely has a plug on the top of its body; remove the plug and screw in the pipe for the showerhead.

Adding a Showerhead

The customer wants a shower installed but wants to keep the old faucet. A special tub spout that had a tap (now capped) was being used for a shower output.

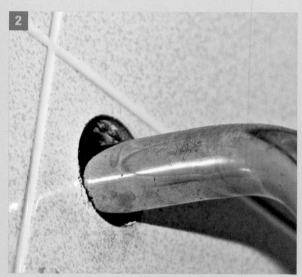

Drill a hole for the showerhead at about 6 ft. 6 in., place blocking behind with winged elbow, screw in showerhead pipe.

The lug on top of the old faucet (*white arrow*) has to be removed so the showerhead pipe can be installed. The flimsy CPVC tub spout pipe (*black arrow*) needs to be replaced with copper or galvanized pipe.

Connect the upper pipe to the drop-ear elbow pipe and install rigid metal pipe for the tub spout. Install the spout on opposite side.

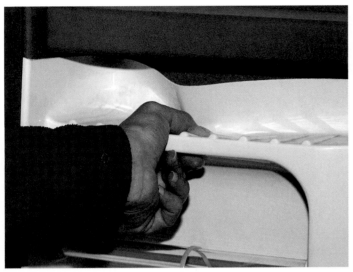

Do the squeeze test. The surround shown at left is too thin; one can easily squeeze it together. But the one at right is rock solid.

Under/Around the Tub

If your remodel includes new flooring, it is best to lay the flooring before installing the tub and sink. That is, extend the flooring all the way under the tub and sink cabinet; this protects the subflooring. This method however, leaves the new floor vulnerable to scuffs and damage as work proceeds, so protect it with a layer of cardboard or several layers of Kraft paper (thick construction paper sold at home centers). Once the tub is in place, protect the tub edge in the same way. I have seen people stand on the tub edge when working overhead and scratch it with their shoes. Where heavy walking is done, put down a carpet runner.

If you do butt new flooring up to the tub, be sure to caulk the tub/flooring interface area with 100 percent clear silicone to keep water from going down under the tub edge.

Tub Surrounds

It used to be that all prefabricated tub surrounds would yellow after a few years, but not any more. Homeowners can now purchase hotel-quality products that are attractive, durable, and easy to clean. One-piece U-shaped surrounds install quickly and are easy to maintain because they are seamless. However, they are often too big to squeeze through a door frame.

Multipiece units—made from a Fiberglas-backed gel-coat, acrylic, or plastic-faced hardboard—are typically composed of three panels that are assembled and glued or nailed onto stud walls. Avoid the thinnest shiny plastic surrounds. To check for quality, pinch the soap holder to see if collapses easily. If it does, the surround is too thin. Look for a thicker model.

If the seams of the surround will be visible, choose one with an imprinted design, such as a tile pattern, that will hide the seams. However, be sure to match the tile grout lines horizontally.

If your surround has a nail-on lip, remember to do just that. Drywall nails work well because they have thin heads that let the wall material lie flat against the nailing lip (as opposed to being pushed off the lip by large-headed screws). Always drill pilot holes first to protect the nail lip from splits or shatters.

For panels that glue on, don't use the adhesive, if any, that comes with the surround. I have seen many panels adhered with that stuff fall off the wall. Instead, use 100 percent clear silicone caulk; once you put the surround up, it stays.

Tileboard is a low-cost watertight surround that glues directly onto drywall or concrete backerboard.

This Tileboard was not caulked at its cut edge on the tub lip. Moisture is entering and its plastic surface is breaking apart as the Tileboard expands.

Solid-surface surrounds vary in price and qualilty. High-end products such as Corian (800-426-7426, www.corian.com) and Swanstone (800-325-7008 www.the swancorp.com) are often used in hotels; they are durable, thick, and easy to clean. Keep the surrounds straight; do not bend them to overlap into a tub or shower lip. Instead, recess the tub or shower base into the stud (by about ¼ in.) so the thick board can go straight down onto the base's lip. Do not put any seams in the shower area, except for the corner.

Tileboard is the inexpensive option. It comes in sheets measuring 4 ft. by 8 ft., priced from $12 per sheet. Tileboard installs onto drywall that has not been taped or finished and may even be on the walls of your remodel. Its advantage is that you can do the entire bath giving it a seamless look from inside the shower to out, it cleans up easily (especially around the light switch), and there are many patterns. On the minus side, any exposed cut edge of the hardboard will absorb water. Wherever the Tileboard has been cut, for example, to accommodate pipes, spouts, and faucet handles, the cut surface must be thoroughly caulked with

100 percent clear silicone to keep out water. Be sure to caulk the edge that abuts the shower or tub base, too. Use 100 percent clear silicone caulk to glue the Tileboard to the drywall. You'll need about one tube per board. For an even better seamless look, install Tileboard along adjoining walls.

Removing an Old Cast-Iron Tub

Removing an old cast-iron tub is no easy task. Breaking it apart is less taxing than removing it in one piece. First disconnect the plumbing and create a clear area. Remove the tile and wallboard above the tub for about 6 in. Then put on gloves and safety glasses and use a sledgehammer to break the tub into pieces small enough to carry out. You might also want to protect the windows with cardboard.

If you want to save the old tub, it is usually possible, but because the tub is so heavy—around 310 lb.—it is a challenge to squeeze it though doorways and other tight places without damaging the floor, doorway, etc. First, disconnect the plumbing and make a clear area around the tub lip. Then break the tub free from anything holding it down. Once it is free, remove the tub with a helper or two, tilting it up to carry it out. This is no task for the weak, the faint-hearted, or those with bad backs.

■ WORK SAFE
■ WORK SMART

If the wall above the tub or shower is going to be tiled, first apply concrete backerboard. Do not use greenboard; it rots like common drywall.

Cutting Surrounds for Windows

Almost any surround or wallboard that glues directly to the wall can be cut for windows. However, solid-surface surrounds are easiest. Measure carefully and, if possible, make a cardboard template. To make a cutout, drill a ⅜-in. hole in each corner and connect the dots with a fine-tooth jigsaw blade. Caulk any exposed edges with 100 percent clear silicone.

If your surround is a thicker, better-quality product, you can use cut pieces for the window sill and window trim or purchase these from the manufacturer. If you're installing low-cost wallboard or an acrylic-type surround, use your home's original trim. Remove the existing trim and cut the surround to fit under the trim and up against the window frame. Then replace the original trim over the surround. If this places the trim "too high," you'll have to butt the wallboard against the trim.

Always drill pilot holes before driving nails or shooting screws through a surround.

Refinishing Your Old Tub

There is a range of choices for refinishing an old tub. If you'd like to do it yourself, you can paint over metal or fiberglass with a high-quality epoxy. First prepare the surface by roughing it up; then clean it. Apply the paint with a brush and wait 5 days before use. You will probably be able to see some brushstrokes on the finish. In some cases, the paint may pull off (for instance, from the stress of a child's suction-cup toy).

Some companies use an acid-etching technique to apply a coating of acrylic. Though it will last a little longer, the end result may be the same as would be achieved by a do-it-yourselfer.

If you are able to remove the tub, you can take it to a refinishing shop where it will be sandblasted, re-enameled on the inside, and painted on the outside. Expect to pay at least $800.

There are also companies that will come to your house and re-glaze the tub using a synthetic aliphatic urethane. They are in and out in 1 day. The typical guarantee is for 10 years. Other companies will come to your home and put an acrylic tub liner over the old tub. I've heard of this process but can't comment on the quality or longevity of the finished product.

Framing In

Carpenters have a one-track mind when it comes to framing: Box the corners and nail a stud every 16 in. This is good as far as it goes, but around a tub/shower enclosure, standard spacing would place a stud in the path of the proposed faucet and water lines. Wherever dead center of the shower faucet is, leave an approximate 14-in. minimum opening without studs (7 in. left and right from dead center—standard stud opening).

Finding dead center on the wall for a tub faucet is easy: Use a level or plumb bob to locate it directly above the tub's drain. A shower-only unit, especially a corner unit, can be less straightforward. Do not measure the wall. Instead, use the shower pan you stand in as a reference. Take a total width measurement of the pan, and then halve that for a centerline reference. Place a light pencil mark dead center on the shower pan (whichever wall you want the faucet to be on), and then use a plumb bob to find the center reference up the length of the wall. The height for a shower-only single-handle faucet should be around waist level; the showerhead should be around 6 ft. 6 in. or higher.

Remember to install a stud for the door frame support (if any). The stud can be nailed to the framing or you can glue it onto the back side of the surround.

If any type of flat wallboard overlaps onto a nailing lip, consider notching the rear studs slightly so the nailing lip will be recessed into the stud wall. This allows the wallboard to extend straight onto the lip without curving. The worst situation is when the base or surround lip lies flat on the stud (not recessed) and large-head screws are used to attach the lip to the stud. Here, you could have the edge of the finished wall bending a full ³⁄₁₆ in. where it lies on the lip.

Tub/Shower Installation

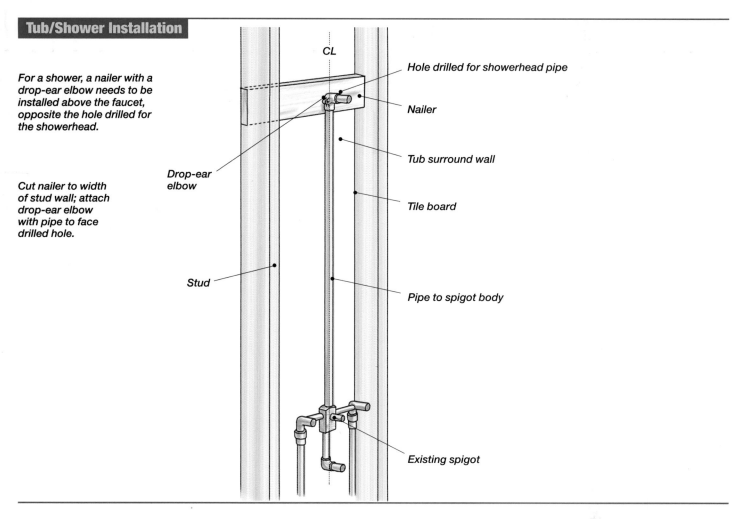

For a shower, a nailer with a drop-ear elbow needs to be installed above the faucet, opposite the hole drilled for the showerhead.

Cut nailer to width of stud wall; attach drop-ear elbow with pipe to face drilled hole.

CL

Hole drilled for showerhead pipe

Nailer

Tub surround wall

Tile board

Drop-ear elbow

Stud

Pipe to spigot body

Existing spigot

Anchoring a Basement Floor Plate

When laying a floor plate on a basement floor be sure to use treated lumber—and cull through the pile at the supply house for straight ones (if the board is slightly bowed, install it with the bow side up). I attach the plate into the floor with masonry screws. To install these, predrill the concrete using the bit that comes with the screws. Be sure you have a masonry bit the correct size for your screws.

1. Cut and lay the 2x4s where the bath is going and get it squared. Mark the floor where the boards are, especially the corners. Do not cut the bottom plate out for the doors. Lay something heavy on the boards so they will not move.

Do not blindly place studs every 16 in. The 16-in. placement in this case forced the plumber to cut out the stud to make room for the faucet.

Single-Handle Faucet

Shown are the typical specs and preparation work for new installation of a single-handle tub/shower faucet. Use galvanized or copper pipe to the tub spout; the pipe to the showerhead can be of any code-approved material.

Height of valve is variable; diameter of hole cut per manufacturer's instructions.

Use plumb bob or level to locate vertical line centered on drain; draw a light pencil line.

Tub/shower drain

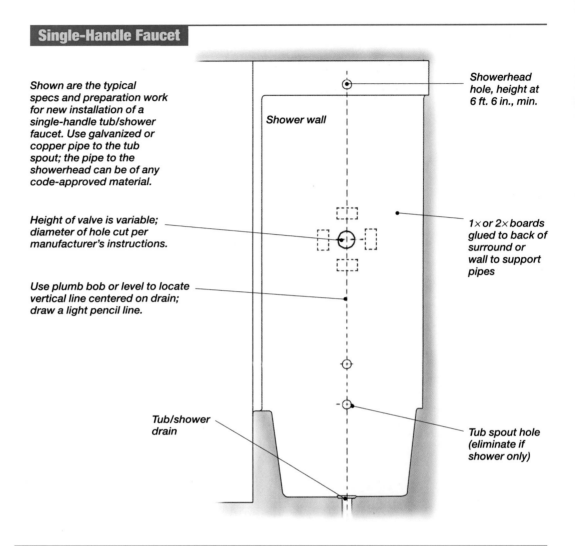

Showerhead hole, height at 6 ft. 6 in., min.

Shower wall

1× or 2× boards glued to back of surround or wall to support pipes

Tub spout hole (eliminate if shower only)

2. Remove each board one at a time and drill holes in the plates with a small twist drill (typically ³⁄₁₆ in.). Drill two holes at each end and then spaced every 2 ft. to 3 ft. Do not drill the plate where the door is going.

3. Lay a board back in position and use a hammer drill to drill starter holes, about ¼ in. deep.

4. Pull the plate back off.

5. Drill each hole at least ½ in. deeper than the screw going into it. Dust will pile around the hole as you drill. You can't do this with the 2x4 plate on top because the concrete dust will refill the hole, blocking the screw. Note, however, that you will never get all the fine dust out of the hole. That's why the drilled hole

should be deeper than the screw length. Without the extra length, the masonry screw will compress and pack the dust (as it screws into the hole), and will stop above the hole bottom, leaving about ¼ in. of the screw head above the plate. Once drilled, blow all the dust away from the hole while the bit is still in the hole. If you do this with the hole open, the dust falls back into the hole, filling it up again (an air compressor works perfectly for this).

Squaring Corners

To lay out for square corners, use sheets of drywall, oriented strand board (OSB), or plywood. Simply lay the sheets on the

Treated Lumber Controversy

In this book, by *treated*, I do not necessarily mean chromated copper arsenate (CCA), often referred to as pressure-treated lumber, which was once commonly available in retail outlets. The CCA mixture contains arsenic, which, according to recent studies, can be absorbed through the skin on contact with the treated wood. Thus when I mention treated wood, I mean whatever safe treatment the industry has switched over to and is currently being sold.

Recessing the shower/tub nailing lip into the stud allows the finished wall (when installed) to fit flush onto the stud as opposed to bending over the lip.

Multi-Handle Faucet

Shown are the typical specs and preparation work for new installation of a two- or three-handle tub/shower faucet. Use galvanized or copper pipe to the tub spout; the pipe to the showerhead can be of any code-approved material.

Shower wall

Showerhead hole, height at 6 ft. 6 in., min.

Draw a light pencil line up from drain center to locate center of spigot and shower head hole.

Use plumb bob or level to locate vertical line centered on drain; draw a light pencil line.

Spigot handle stem

Spigot body

Galvanized or copper pipe for tub spout, if any

Use level and pencil to draw a light pencil line across the tub face at proposed height of spigot handles.

Distance per manufacturer's instructions

Tub/shower drain

---

floor and trace around them. Or if you are going to install tiles on the floor, do this first. Use the tiles as reference lines for your layout.

Sometimes a wall has to go at a specific spot, in which case it is your reference. Lay that wall first. Then butt the 4x8 references against that one floor plate to form the rest of the bath's sides. Or lay the floor tile with that one wall as a reference and stop the tile where you want the wall to be placed. The wall can be placed on top of vinyl tile, but not ceramic. Do not lay a wall on top vinyl tile where the tile does not extend all the way under the plate; you don't want the wall tilting.

Working with Walls or Floors That Are out of Plumb

Often with remodel plumbing, existing walls and floors are out of plumb, out of level, or just downright crooked. If you have unlevel floor joists, attach new straight "sister" joists against the old ones, slightly higher, to create a new flat floor. If you are out of level with the door threshold, you will have to taper to the threshold or use the threshold as your finished floor reference and scab on your new joists so as to be parallel to the

Installing ceramic floor tile over a wood subfloor almost guarantees cracking because joists flex as you walk on them, but tile does not.

threshold (via the finished floor, not the floor joists themselves).

Framing Screws Are Better Than Nails

In a remodel, you may change your plans as the job proceeds and as you encounter problems. For that reason, whenever possible I frame with long drywall screws rather than nails. That way, I can easily remove and reposition a stud without destroying it. Using nails means hammer banging—and trash raining down in your eyes (not to mention snakes and spiders falling from above), and the possibility of taking a stud out of plumb. Of course, using a framing and finish nail gun is the fastest way to do any construction, but most plumbers don't have these. When attaching a new stud or joist against another, I predrill a small hole through the first stud, and then shoot in the screw. It quickly passes through the first stud and threads its way into the second. This also allows me to fine-tune the plumb of the stud or joist since I can easily pull the screw, readjust, and shoot it in again. Oh, did I mention this is a heck of a lot quieter!

Leveling the Floor

Attaching sister joists to the old joists is one way to level the floor.

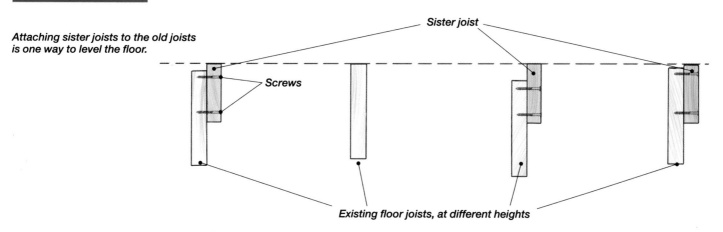

Sister joist

Screws

Existing floor joists, at different heights

All About Toilet Seats

You might expect that buying a new toilet seat would be a simple decision, but at a home center or plumbing store, you will find a wall full of choices: cushioned, painted wood, oak, plastic, round, oval, color, custom color, metal hinge, slow close, plastic hinge, pull out, etc. You can even special-order a heated seat.

Check whether your toilet bowl is round or oval, and get a seat of the same shape. Lengths sometimes vary, so I measure the existing toilet from the hinge to the bowl front edge, and check this against the items on display. Generally, thick plastic seats with plastic hinges are preferable to wood seats with metal hinges. Oak seats tend to split, painted wood seats tend to disintegrate, and metal hinges corrode quickly.

Look at the method of hinge attachment to bowl to verify how hard it will be to install. Be sure the seat legs—the little bumpers that rest on the bowl—are solid plastic; if they are hollow, they will crack and break. If needed, these pieces can be purchased separately and glued or nailed onto the seat bottom. If your toilet is a special color, you will probably have to get the toilet seat from the same manufacturer to be sure it matches.

You get what you pay for. Painted wood seats disintegrate around the edge where urine collects. This seat is only 1 year old.

Metal hinges, even chrome or even brass, corrode from the day they are installed. This one is less than 1 year old.

Picking a Toilet

When 1.6-gal. flushes were first introduced, some manufacturers opted to retain the same design and simply reduce the water per flush. This didn't work. One manufacturer's toilet had to have the handle held down for the entire flush cycle; another manufacturer sent out letters of apology. Now, however, the 1.6-gal. toilet designs work well; and as each year passes, the designs get better and better. The model I prefer is American Standard's Champion. Following is a discussion of what I look for when buying a toilet.

ELONGATED (OVAL) BOWL In my opinion, the elongated shape is more stylish, comfortable, and sanitary than a round bowl. The elongated bowl will extend out from the wall 2 in. farther than a round bowl (which will typically extend out 28⅜ in.).

FULLY GLAZED, LARGE-DIAMETER TRAPWAY The trapway is where water flows within the toilet when it is flushed. "Fully glazed" means the entire waterway, not just the visible outside surface, is smooth and glazed. When the trapway is only partially glazed, rough areas grow rougher over time, with stalactites sticking out and grabbing all that flows. If your toilet is relatively new and constantly plugging up, this may be your problem. Also, make sure that the trapway is at least 2 in. in diameter. American Standard's Champion toilet has the largest trapway I know of: 2⅜ in.

QUIET, SMOOTH. FULL FLUSH You don't want a noisy toilet. This is normally not a problem unless you get a pressure-assisted toilet. They are quite noisy, but they work well. If this is what you want, consider insulating the bathroom walls.

One toilet that flushes well: the American Standard Champion.

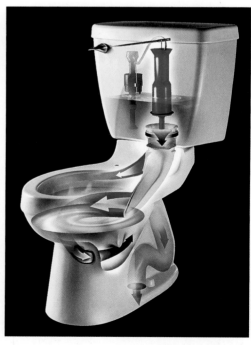

Water travels quickly through a fully glazed trapway, creating a fast, efficient flush.

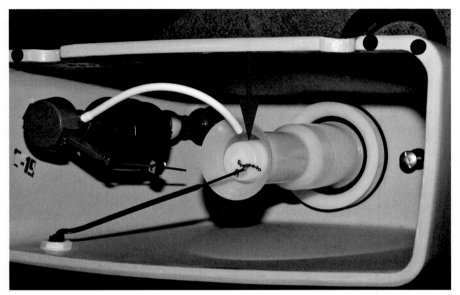

The Champion tank has an extra-large 2⅜-in. flush valve opening, which efficiently dumps water into the bowl for a fast, smooth flush.

A large-diameter trapway is the key to preventing blockage. At 2⅛ in., this is one of the largest available. Don't settle for anything less than 2 in.

EXTRA-LARGE FLUSH VALVE The flush valve is the opening that dumps water into the bowl from the tank and flushes everything away. The larger the hole, the better. American Standard's Champion toilet has a 3-in. opening, a full inch wider than the typical valve diameter.

MASS A heavier unit has more china content and, consequently, a more solid, quality feel. Low-cost units cut corners and have less china.

STYLE AND COLOR Classic white goes with anything and is available in styles to match any decor. Special colors tend to be discontinued after a few years and may be difficult to match when something breaks or the rest of the bath is remodeled.

To speed up water flow from the tank into the bowl, this model (American Standard Champion) uses a smooth plastic water diverter; it rapidly delivers water to various orifices within the bowl.

TANK/BOWL DESIGN Most toilets come in two pieces—a tank and a bowl. Older one-piece toilets had a low tank that was approximately the height of the bowl—a design with numerous problems. Today's one-piece models have a high tank and bowl molded in one piece, a design that is easy to clean. The newest two-piece models are nearly seamless.

SEAT HEIGHT FROM FLOOR The standard height of a toilet is around 15 in. from the floor. Most adults are comfortable with a bit more height, around 16½ in.

INSULATED TANK An insulated tank prevents water condensation on the outside surface of the tank. However, the bowl will still sweat.

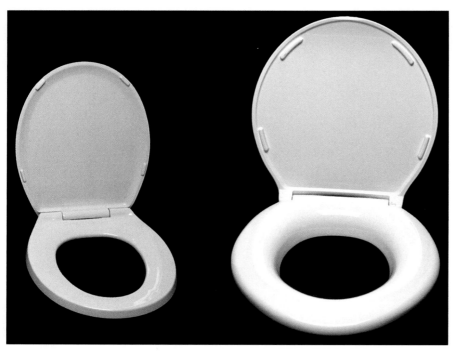

The typical toilet seat (*at left*) can be a literal pain in the butt as it has not evolved to fit modern humans. Big John (*at right*) is designed for today's larger framed bodies.

Picking a toilet seat

By far, the best designed, most comfortable toilet seat has to go to Big John—the new lid on the market (www.bigjohntoiletseat.com, 866-366-0669). As humans evolve, we have expanded in almost every dimension—as made obvious by watching almost any sport (or diet commercial). The toilet seat, however, has not evolved with us. Simply put, we need a larger seat.

Enter Big John. A stylish ergonomic design with 4 in. more sitting room, it has a 2½ in. wider opening and is 2⅜ in. taller than a standard seat. Made from antimicrobial plastic, this larger, more comfortable seat will fit the posterior contour of the most discriminating user. But the design doesn't stop there. The hinge mechanism is stainless steel and under the seat are extremely large "rubber bumpers" that grip the porcelain to keep the seat from shifting.

Pulling a Toilet

Pulling a toilet is normally a simple job, but there are several steps.

1. Verify that the new toilet is the right color and type, and is in good condition (check for hairline cracks). Have as much of it preassembled as you want.
2. Check the floor. If the floor around the toilet is spongy, you may have to reinforce it or replace rotted wood. In worst-case situations, I've also had to replace the joists underneath. On one job where the floor joists were rotted away in the dirt underneath, I had to pour a mini concrete pad to support the toilet. The irony is that, once done, the toilet was the only

stable thing in a house that would move with the wind.

3. Measure from the finished wall. The distance to the toilet hold-down bolts on the floor from the finished wall should be 12 in. If this distance varies beyond 1 in., someone screwed up the installation, and you may find that a common 12-in. rough-in toilet will not fit (assuming a new toilet is going back in). Most manufacturers stock 10-in. and 14-in. rough-in toilets. For these, colors may have to be special ordered. At least one manufacturer makes a model that converts on site.

4. Check the existing bowl and tank for cracks. If there are cracks, the bowl/tank may break apart in your hands as you pull. Shards are razor sharp, so be sure to wear protective gloves and clothing.

5. Turn off the toilet's stop valve.

6. Disconnect the supply tube either from the stop valve or at the toilet.

7. Flush to get rid of the water. Hold down the lever to rid the toilet of as much water as possible. Remove any residual water from the bowl and tank. Use an old towel for the tank and use a plastic margarine tub for the bowl.

8. Plan where you'll put the old toilet. Will you duck-walk it out immediately? If so, put down a carpet runner to protect the floor, and open the door. If you plan to set the toilet aside when it's first pulled, place a sheet of thick plastic or cardboard nearby. If the cardboard is thick enough, you can pull the old toilet outside on the cardboard. Be careful that the old wax seal on the toilet's underside does not touch a finished floor.

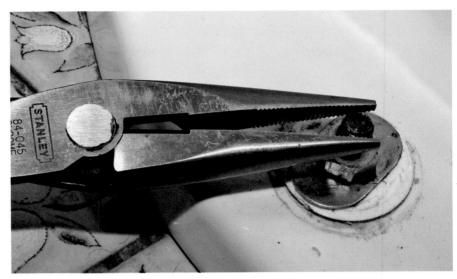

If the bowl hold-down bolt spins as you attempt to loosen the nut, hold on to the upper part of the bolt with needle-nose pliers.

A Makita mini reciprocating saw has a thin blade and tiny teeth that are perfect for cutting free a toilet bolt.

9. Keep supplies handy. Helpful things to have on hand include new toilet bolts and a new wax seal (or two), a towel to plug the hole (to keep sewer gas from entering the house), paper towels and a garbage bag, rubber gloves, and antiseptic mouthwash (to rinse hands and arms when done).

10. Unscrew the two hold-down nuts. Removing the nuts from the bolts holding the toilet to the floor is sometimes a problem. If a bolt spins as you turn the nut, you'll have to

■ WORK SAFE
■ WORK SMART

Cold wax does not squish well, which may cause a problem when setting the toilet in place. If the wax seal has been stored in a cold place, bring it inside and warm it up to room temperature before installing.

figure out some way to hold the bolt so it won't spin. If there is enough bolt showing above the nut, you can hold it with needle-nose pliers. If not, you will have to cut the bolt where it goes through the bowl foot. A mini-reciprocating saw with a fine-tooth blade will cut through the bolt in seconds.

However, this tool and its blades may be hard to find locally, and its brittle blades break easily. You can use a hacksaw; it may take forever or a few seconds. Cutting time will depend on how much room you have to move the saw back and forth (always use a fresh, sharp blade). Be careful not to scratch the porcelain unless you are throwing the toilet away. A friend of mine has good luck in cutting straight down through the nut (not the bolt) vertically, rather than horizontally.

11. Pull the toilet straight up.

12. Check the location of the old wax seal. If it did not come off with the toilet, remove it from the toilet flange. Pliers work fine for this. Put the seal straight into a garbage bag or place it out of the way on some paper towels.

13. Look at the flange. If the bolt attachment points are rusted away, you will have to install a special flange designed to mount over the old one or use wood-screw hold-down bolts, assuming a new toilet is going back in.

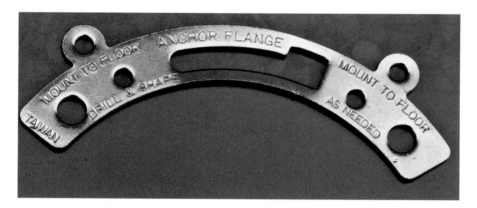

All these toilet flanges are designed to fit flush to the floor (over broken and rusted-out flanges) and give toilet bowl bolts something to attach to.

Installing a Toilet

Installing a toilet can be easy or hard. Often the $50 cheap-o toilets are hardest to install because they may not be flat on the bottom and probably have none of the tank hardware preinstalled.

When a customer wants to choose a toilet for me to install, I always tell him or her that I will install it by the hour, not at a preset price. I know how long it takes to install the toilet I recommend: just a few minutes. Another toilet may take all day. One customer chose a toilet that had a hairline mold crack in the tank, which was not detected until the installation was complete (late morning), including water in the tank. He had to pay me by the hour to remove it and wait for him to return with a replacement. The second one also had a mold fault in the bowl. By the time he got back with the third toilet, I was having dinner with his family.

1. Verify that the old wax seal and plastic funnel, if any, have been removed from the toilet flange.
2. Verify that the wood around the toilet is not rotten. The old flange must be secure and able to accept new flange bolts.
3. Verify the floor is level or you may have to shim the toilet bowl. I've had floors so unlevel that I had to split the difference between the floor and the tank/bowl interface. You do this by tightening one tank hold-down bolt more than the other. However, gaps of more than ¼ in. are noticeable. Rather than do this, you may to have to create a floor shim from treated wood or leftover tile.
4. Install the new flange bolts. Be sure they are aligned at the exact center of the flange, parallel to the wall. Lock them in place via a washer and nut on top of the flange. You do not

Safety Tips When Pulling a Toilet

■ Do not rub your eyes or face during this process.

■ Be careful when pulling toilets that are cracked; they may break in your hands with edges that are razor sharp.

■ Do not lift the toilet if you have a bad back.

■ You need not remove the bowl lid unless it is going to be re-used.

want them to fall over as you lower the bowl.

5. Flip the bowl over and install a new wax seal on the toilet horn. Use a funnel-type seal. If the old flange is below the finished floor by ¾ in. or more, install a funnel-type seal on the flange (rather than on the toilet horn) and a wax ring with no funnel on top of that.
6. Check the alignment. Pick up the bowl and raise it over the toilet flange, aligning the center of the bowl with the center of the flange. Align the two flange bolts with the bolt slots in the bowl feet. Slowly lower the bowl straight down onto the bolts.
7. You should feel the wax ring squishing down on the flange. Keep pushing and rocking the bowl until the bowl is touching the floor. If you have trouble squishing it down, sit on the bowl and rock a bit to help seat it into position.
8. Align the bowl so that it faces straight forward.
9. Place a level across the bowl to verify that it is not tilted. Shim if necessary.
10. Insert washers over the flange bolts (and optional cap fasteners), and tighten down via the proper diameter nut. Do not over-tighten or you may break the bowl's feet. Check tightness by trying to gently rock

WHAT CAN GO WRONG

If the finished bath flooring was installed around the old toilet (and not under), some unfinished flooring may be visible beneath the new toilet if the new toilet footprint doesn't match the old.

WHAT CAN GO WRONG

You over-tighten tank bolts or toilet flange bolts, which causes the toilet to break.

WHAT CAN GO WRONG

You clean an old, cold toilet tank by pouring in a hot-water solution. The tank will pop (break) sounding like a rifle being shot. This is a mistake I made only once.

the bowl. If you feel it move, tighten some more—but be sure it was the bowl that moved and not the floor or flange.

11. If necessary, cut off any excess bolt above the nut. Install the caps. I normally ignore proprietary methods for installing caps. I simply fill a cap with plumber's putty and insert it over the bolt and nut.

12. Install the tank on the bowl. Typically, you have to place a spud washer (large circular foam gasket) on the tank's flush valve (the large threaded thing sticking out its bottom). Then turn the tank over, centering a spud washer on the bowl's water inlet hole (behind where the lid attaches), and set the tank onto the bowl. Verify that the rubber washer is on the tank bolt. Tighten it down via the tank bolts and nuts. Do not over-tighten, but make sure the tank can't rock or swivel.

13. You may or may not have to assemble the mechanisms inside the tank, depending on manufacturer.

Bathroom Sinks

If you're shopping for a new bathroom sink, your basic choice will be between storage and openness. The common vanity offers a bit of storage, and protects young children from the plumbing below. The classic pedestal sink has an open design with visible plumbing; several modern sink-bowl-only styles also expose the plumbing.

When choosing a desk-style vanity, pay attention to the drawers and where they open. Occasionally, a drawer will be located where the drain or water line needs to be.

Install as large a vanity as space permits, leaving at least 15 in. from the side of the vanity to the center of the toilet; 18 in. is more comfortable. Installing a vanity is usually simple work: Just slide the unit against the wall and hook up the plumbing. But avoid sliding the unit flush into a corner. Though the base of the unit will fit nicely, the top usually will have a 1-in. lip overhanging the base on either side. Thus in a corner if the base and top are butted to the wall, the top will be off-center.

Some things to keep in mind when you install a vanity:

- The cabinet may or may not have a back.
- Install the room's trim after the vanity goes in, and bump it against the vanity side.
- The drywall behind the vanity does not have to be finished or even painted. But if during a later remodel you replace the vanity with a smaller unit, the paint discrepancy will be noticeable.
- Choose a vanity with no front post between the doors. The post is not needed and gets in the way of installing and maintaining the plumbing.
- Consider installing a piece of scrap vinyl on the floor of the vanity cabinet where water normally drips.
- Install the bath floor before the sink goes in.
- If two bowls are in one sink cabinet and are only a couple of feet apart, use only one trap. If separated by several feet, come out of the wall for each sink and use separate traps.

Pedestal Sink

There is something classy about a pedestal sink. A century ago, pedestal sinks were made of enameled cast iron. By 1915, vitreous china, a glass-like porcelain (glazed clay baked for 40 hours in a 2,200° kiln), became the material of choice. Enameled cast-iron pedestal sinks are still available in antique shops and many sell for a hefty sum.

Basically, a pedestal sink is a wall sink. It uses the same type of wall bracket with a single, center leg (the pedestal) adding support underneath. Wall-hung sinks without legs have a tendency to pull down from the front.

The challenge with a pedestal sink is installing the plumbing neatly, since it will be visible. The pictures you see in catalogs generally don't show the drain or water pressure lines. If the pedestal is wide, you may be able to hide the plumbing behind and within it.

The difference between a quality sink and a low-cost sink is generally the mass (vitreous china) in both the pedestal and the basin. I've seen pedestal sinks so low in mass (and so narrow) that the pedestal could not stand on its own; the sink would tilt if you leaned on the front left or right corner. Often these sinks require added support via thin metal legs on the two front corners of the basin.

Typically, a pedestal sink has an angled back that slides down onto one or two angle brackets mounted to the wall. There should be a horizontal nailer or blocker board behind the finished wall; the bracket is attached by driving screws into the nailer (as is done for a common wall-hung sink installation). The pedestal supports the sink center. The sink shown on p. 152 has a flat underside (where the sink meets the wall) that rests on a ¾-in. board mounted to the wall and secured through the drywall to the nailer behind. The two back corners of the sink are secured to the nailer via lag screws; this pulls the sink tight against the wall. I must say I prefer this installation over the slide-in angle-bracket system. The angle-bracket system sometimes allows the sink to tilt and move.

Whatever model you install, have the sink on site before you install the plumbing. Read through the plumbing instructions below before you start because the drain and water lines must be installed with precision at or around the center leg, so that they will be hidden

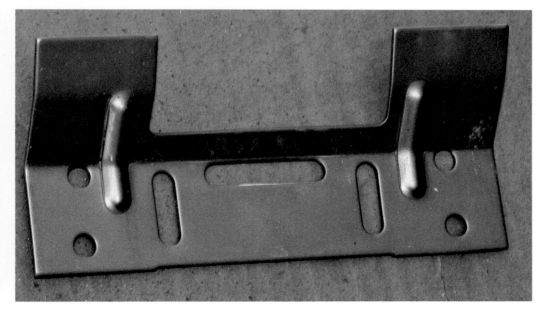

A lighter-weight pedestal sink uses a wall attachment bracket, rather than a board, to support the sink back. It must also be attached to blocking within the wall.

Prep Work for a Pedestal Sink

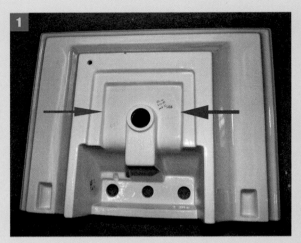

Flip the pedestal sink basin over and determine where the pedestal leg is going to fit onto it.

Assemble the sink against the wall where it is to be installed.

Mark the stud where the bottom of the sink basin touches it (measure this mark to the floor).

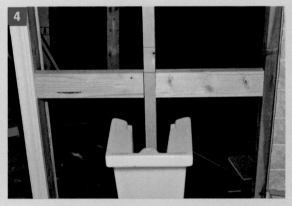

Insert nailers (blocking) between the studs, using your mark as a center reference.

Once the finished wall is up, attach a support board to the previously measured height reference. This holds the rear of the pedestal sink. Some sinks use a metal bracket instead.

Pedestal Sink Drain Line

For finished wall with access to an open wall behind: Drill a 2-in. hole for an incoming 1½-in. drain pipe. The bottom of drilled hole is parallel to the bottom of the basin drain pipe.

For an unfinished wall: The bottom of the new 1½-in. drain pipe must be parallel to the bottom of the tailpiece.

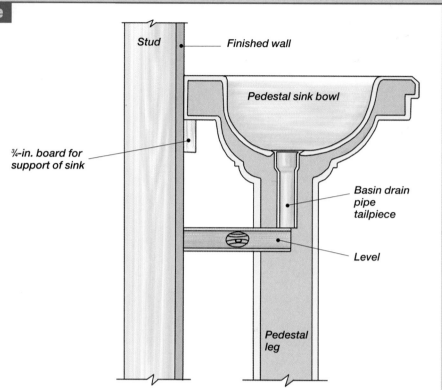

Stud

Finished wall

Pedestal sink bowl

¾-in. board for support of sink

Basin drain pipe tailpiece

Level

Pedestal leg

Drop-Ear Elbow Fitting

A drop-ear elbow allows you to make a 90° turn within the wall and to connect a nonmetal pipe to a copper pipe at the point of use.

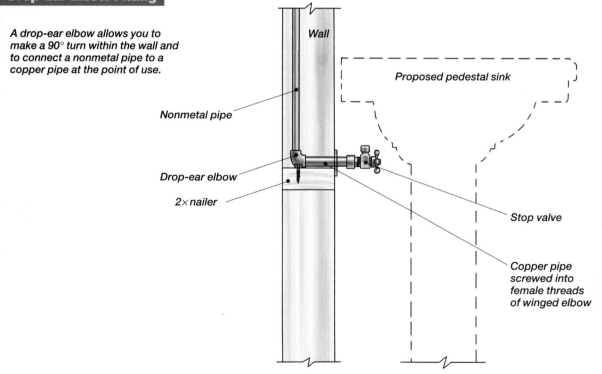

Wall

Proposed pedestal sink

Nonmetal pipe

Drop-ear elbow

2× nailer

Stop valve

Copper pipe screwed into female threads of winged elbow

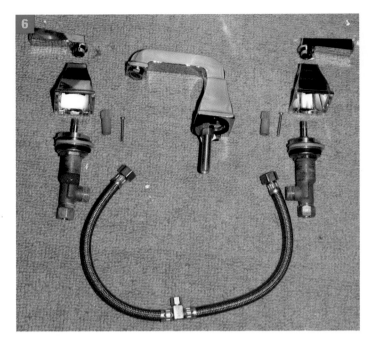

Flip the sink and install the faucet before you install the sink. Underneath, loop the excess pipe between the faucet center and the side inlets.

When installing widespread faucets, it always helps to first lay out the pieces on a flat surface and figure out which part goes where.

Jam a piece of wood against the side outlet nut to keep the faucet handle body from moving as you tighten the supply tube nut.

from view as much as possible and so that they will fit onto the sink.

You will not be able to remove a vanity sink unit and install a pedestal sink without reworking the plumbing and installing a support bracket in the wall.

1. Install the faucet, insert the supply tubes, and install the drain tailpiece onto the sink (or basin) as soon as it comes out of the box. Set the sink and the pedestal leg in place. Do not let it fall over.

2. Mark the stud or wall to indicate where the nailer needs to be to support the sink back. Take a measurement from the floor to the top of the sink ledge where the support board or metal bracket is to meet the sink ledge. Install a 2x10 across two stud widths inside the wall. Install a smaller board only if you are certain that you don't need a wider board to add some tolerance.

3. Finish and trim the wall.

4. Set the sink in its proposed location (against the wall), and mark the wall where the support board (or metal wedge support) needs to go. Verify that it does not go too far left or

right and that it will fit into what-ever recess the sink has made for it. Double-check the height via the measurement taken in Step 2.

5. Remove the sink and the pedestal leg, and screw in a short ¾-in. board (or a metal bracket) along the mark.

6. From the bottom of the basin drain-pipe, use a small level, and make a plumb mark on the finished wall directly behind the pipe. This will be the bottom of the 2-in. hole you need to drill for the incoming 1½-in. drain line.

7. Bring just enough pipe out from the finished wall to glue into the hub of a trap adapter. Be sure you have an escutcheon (flange) that will fit over the pipe.

8. Attach the P-trap to the basin drain-pipe (cutting any extra length off its arm), and insert the P-trap arm into the drain as you set the basin on the ¾-in. board. Though one person can

do this, it's a lot easier with two people.

9. Slide the pedestal leg in place. Align the pedestal, and tighten the nut on the trap adapter.

10. Lock the corners of the sink to the wall using lag screws. Be careful not to over-tighten lest you break the china. I sometimes use a rubber washer (toilet tank hold-down bolt washer).

11. If the floor is not plumb, you may need to shim the leg.

Rough-In Plumbing Only

If you are doing rough-in plumbing work only, be sure to allow for the thickness of the finished wall (typically ½-in. drywall). Run the drain line through the wall before the finished wall goes in, and be sure it is in the exact required location. Add the wall bracket after the finished wall is in place, then install the drain.

Shoot lag screws through the bottom left and right edge of the sink basin into blocking within the wall.

Set the sink basin onto the leg. Verify that the leg is properly centered within the basin slot. The back of the basin must be against the wall, supported by the wallboard.

A sweat-to-fit drop-ear elbow fitting makes a good transition fitting from nonmetallic pipe to a copper stubout. The nailer is mounted flat between two studs.

If copper pipe was used throughout, use a copper sweat-on (both sides) drop-ear elbow.

Extend the copper pipe through the wall adjacent to the fixture where the stop needs to be located.

Slide on the escutcheon and cut the copper pipe to length, about 3 in. out from the finished wall.

Installing the Stops

Stop valves for both under the sink and under the toilet install in the same way. The pipe going to the stop needs to be anchored so the pipe does not swivel as you turn the stop on and off. For an all-copper installation, use a sweat-in/sweat-out drop-ear elbow fitting that screws to a nailer. CPVC and PEX require drop-ear elbows that interface their pipe to female threads. CPVC drop-ear elbows come with a union where the pipe glues into the fitting. Attach this type of drop-ear elbow onto the nailer so that you can get a pipe wrench onto the union collar in case you need to tighten it further after the nailer has been installed.

1. Find the location where the stop is to be mounted and attach a 2x4 or 2x6 nailer between the studs within the wall directly behind.
2. Drill a hole (⁹⁄₁₆ in. for copper, ¾ in. for galvanized) in the finished wall exactly behind where the stop will be adjacent to the fixture.
3. Mount a drop-ear elbow on the nailer precisely positioned behind the drilled hole in the finished wall.
4. Sweat a male adapter onto a short section of copper pipe. Screw this into the drop-ear elbow. You can also use galvanized pipe with brass, gold, or a chrome finish. Or paint the galvanized the same color as the bath wall.
5. Stick the pipe through the wall, and secure the nailer between the studs.
6. Cut pipe to the length needed—typically 3 in. to 4 in. beyond the finished wall. For galvanized, you must use the proper length nipple.
7. Slide on the escutcheon and sweat (or screw) the stop onto the pipe. Make sure you do not damage anything with the heat or flame.

Grab Bars

Grab bars, long associated with institutional settings, are now commonly installed in homes, and for good reason. Slipping in the tub, shower, or on a wet tile floor is a real hazard for everyone, not just the elderly. Grab bars provide a safety net for all of us.

A shower stall grab bar should be mounted 36 in. to 48 in. from the floor, and a tub/shower grab bar 24 in. to 48 in. For new construction, simply span a 2x6 nailer, or blocking, from stud to stud across the area where the flange will be mounted. If the wall is already up, standard practice is to shoot two of the three screws (a bar flange has three screw holes for mounting) into a stud to a depth of at least 1 in., and to use a plastic anchor for the third. Having two of the three screws solidly anchored will exceed the minimum required rating of 250 lb. Use #12 screws (or larger) that are at least 1¾ in. long.

Grab bar designs range from simple to complex. A vertical bar mounted at the entrance usually works best for people who need help getting in and out of the bath or shower. A horizontal bar is best for people who stand up as they shower, and a diagonal bar helps those who sit down to get back up. And, of course, you can have all three in one bar. You can order showers with grab bars already installed as part of the surround—such as the Lasco Freedom series. These bars are 36 in. from the floor.

Bar diameters vary, too. The smaller the diameter, the better the grip for fingers, but strength is somewhat sacrificed. Use large-diameter bars where a bather needs to pull up to a standing position, and use the smaller-diameter bars for everything else.

Splitting a flame shield and sliding it onto the pipe allows the shield to fully surround the fitting to be sweated, and protects the wall.

Remove the shield, attach the supply tube, and you're done. This, obviously, has to be done for both hot and cold.

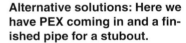

Alternative solutions: Here we have PEX coming in and a finished pipe for a stubout.

CHAPTER 6

The Utility Room and Basement

THE UTILITY ROOM/ basement is often the "catch-all" plumbing area of the house. Things that don't fit elsewhere are usually installed here.

Typically, if the basement is unfinished, the pipes for the first floor are openly visible in the basement, overhead in the floor joists. This arrangement provides easy access to pipes for first-floor fixtures, but it's a headache for adding new plumbing service, such as a toilet, to the basement. This chapter will show you how to solve that problem, with lots of illustrations from a real-life service call where we put a toilet in a basement with all pipes overhead.

We will also install a whole-house cartridge filter to solve the family's problem with iron in the water. As simple as you might think these to be, most cartridge filters are installed wrong. They also are made in poor designs as well as good. During the install, I will show you how to pick a good design and how to install one properly, taking maintenance into consideration.

Many readers have requested information on installing a booster pump, so we will take you along on a service call where we do just that.

A basement toilet can be installed even if the pipes are overhead. From the bathroom perspective, you have no idea there is a pumping system in use.

Finally, we will show how to increase your hot water supply by installing a second water heater, either in series with or parallel to the existing heater. This upgrade is popular among families with a lot of kids, but it's also appreciated by those who enjoy a hefty supply of hot water for showering pleasure.

Installing a Cartridge Water Filter

Adding a cartridge filter to improve water quality is probably the most common plumbing add-on. It can solve myriad problems, ranging from sediment to odor. The plumbing work is simple and inexpensive, but it's important to choose a good cartridge housing to avoid pitfalls, which include leaks and difficulty replacing cartridges. Here's what to look for.

THREADING There should be metal female pipe threads where the incoming

Leak at the Cartridge Filter Housing

When I find a persistent leak at the housing's plastic threaded female joint that cannot be stopped (the housing has no brass insert or washer), I take a plastic threaded nipple, put glue on the threads, and then screw it in the plastic housing. Once the glue sets up, it fuses the pipe nipple into the housing's threads, and the leak is no more.

and outgoing water pipes attach to the filter. Better filters often have threaded brass sleeves. Plastic female threads tend to leak, especially if a pipe has already cut threads deep into the housing. If metal threads are impossible to find, a second option is a design that has a washer hose gasket on the inside of the female threads.

INTERNAL SHUT-OFF VALVES When you replace the filter in the basement, you don't want to be greeted by a flood

Adding a Cartridge Filter

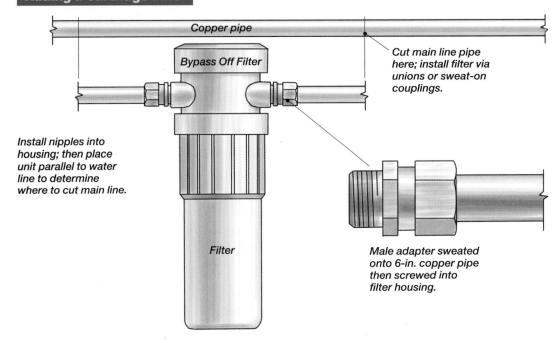

Copper pipe

Bypass Off Filter

Cut main line pipe here; install filter via unions or sweat-on couplings.

Install nipples into housing; then place unit parallel to water line to determine where to cut main line.

Filter

Male adapter sweated onto 6-in. copper pipe then screwed into filter housing.

Extending the Life of a Carbon Filter

You can extend the life of a carbon filter by putting a string filter in front of it to remove the large sediments and by using larger or dual cartridges. Professional suppliers stock 20-in. vertical housings that stack one common 10-in. cartridge on top of the other (or use a single 20-in cartridge, which you also buy from them). You don't save any money, but it doubles the time between cartridge replacements.

Removing Lead from Your Home's Water

Lead in a home's water supply is a growing concern. Lead is toxic even in small amounts and because it is heavy, the body stores it. The safety limit is 0 ppb (parts per billion), and the legal limit is 10 ppb to 15 ppb. Since lead particles are so small, it's hard to filter them all out and difficult to gauge how successful a filter is. Granulated activated carbon (GAC) cartridges (not block carbon) may remove some lead, but not all. Some manufacturers are treating their carbon cartridges to make them more suitable for lead removal. GAC systems claim to remove lead with 1 micron to 0.5 micron filtering. Systems that are certified by a state or federal agency are considered reliable. For more information, see www.nsf.org/certified/dwtu/.

of water as you remove the old filter. If your filter doesn't have internal valves, you can install ball valves on the water line separately; good ball valves cost about $12 each.

The filter head should have three positions: bypass, off, and filter (or the equivalent). When turned to "off," no water can drain out onto you and the floor via the water lines if you remove the cartridge. That is, both valves (incoming and outgoing) in the filter's head are turned off by rotating the head of the filter. No water will flow into the housing either. "Filter" means that the water is flowing through the filter cartridge. "Bypass" means that water is flowing through the filter head but not through the cartridge. If the filter ever plugs up—stopping all the water going into the house—turning the filter head to the "bypass" position will let unfiltered water into the house.

CARTRIDGE HOUSING Look for a design that allows for easy removal of the cartridge housing and doesn't let you easily lose the O-ring. You may want to lubricate the seal with plumber's grease or Vaseline. This keeps the O-ring from bunching up and tearing as the housing is screwed back onto the head.

EXTRA O-RING SEALS It's easy to lose or damage an O-ring seal during a filter change, so keep an extra one nearby. If you lose the O-ring and have no spare, turn the filter head to "bypass" to get water back to the house

SPECIAL HANDLE A special handle to aid in loosening the cartridge housing is a good idea. Sometimes this will come with the filter system; other times it must be bought. Be sure to hang it adjacent to the filter in a visible location.

Filter Material

Though filter material varies to target different elements, the cartridge housing is basically the same. The housing holds any of a number of different types of cartridges. The most popular cartridges are carbon, string, and pleated paper. For all of these (and for any filter), it is imperative that you have a schedule for replacement. A cartridge left in the housing for several years gives bacteria a good place to grow and is asking for trouble. It's not a good idea to leave a cartridge in place for more than 1 year. A typical replacement schedule for 10-in. cartridges is once per month or every other month.

CARBON Carbon filters remove sediment, chlorine, and organic chemicals and improve the taste and odor of the house water. Carbon block cartridges (solid like a rock) are cheaper than activated carbon cartridges (powder). However, they clog quickly and remove fewer particles from the water. All carbon filters are rated for micron filtering (filtering the smallest particles). The higher the rating number, the longer the filter will last (and the less it will cost), but the fewer particles it will filter. This basic principle applies to all filters. There's always a trade-off between longevity (and cost) versus cleaning. A 50-micron filter removes only the largest contaminants, while a 5-micron filter removes most sediment, iron, and some lead. A 0.5-micron filter removes just about everything, but clogs up very quickly. Most people compromise with a 5-micron filter.

STRING String cartridges are manufactured from a durable polypropylene cord that is wound around a rigid polypropylene core. They are fairly economical (a step up from the pleated paper filter) and reduce sediment, sand, silt, rust, and scale particles. They are advertised to filter out particles as small as 5 microns, but iron particles that do not get through a 5-micron carbon filter will still get through a 5-micron string cartridge. So it's not much help for removing dissolved iron.

PLEATED PAPER Pleated paper (cellulose) cartridges are popular due to their low cost. They filter out sediment down

Mounting Brackets for the Cartridge Filter Housing

If you have flexible pipe, you must mount the filter housing securely, using brackets, so that it will not be stressed when the cartridge is being changed. If the main water line is metal, brackets are optional, depending how secure and "locked down" the pipe is. After many years, a few manufacturers have figured this out and are supplying brackets with the filter; however, these brackets are often thin and cheap. The best brackets are common angle brackets sold at the hardware store. You will also need two U-shaped bolts to hold the pipe to the bracket. Instead of brackets, I've also substituted 2x4s nailed to joists.

to about 20 microns, which is about half the size of visible particles. I don't recommend them because I've seen many disintegrate and send paper throughout the water system. A pleated polyester cartridge that is reusable is available, but it is normally sold only at professional dealers.

Planning a Location

Once you've decided to install a cartridge filter, the first decision is where to put it. Take a look at the area where the main water line pipe comes into the house; you'll need an accessible spot in this area. Determine where you are going to cut the pipe, what tools you will need, and the pipe and fittings needed to travel to where the filter will be mounted and back.

If you are in the country and use a water pressure tank, it is best to install the filter after the tank—not before—because if the filter plugs up, the pressure switch will read this as a lack of water pressure in the house and will refuse to turn off. This, in turn, may blow a fitting off the water line since a submersible pump can raise several hundred pounds of pressure.

Choosing and Mounting a Cartridge Filter

Visualize what the end product will look like, and pick a location where it will fit. Common angle brackets work well to secure a cartridge filter.

A good attachment method: Screw ¾-in. galvanized nipples into the filter head, which are secured by U-brackets onto the angle brackets.

A filter head with built-in valves will have three positions, as this one does.

Filters with metal female threads tend to leak less than filters with plastic threads.

With the filter securely mounted, you can unscrew the housing and insert a cartridge. Be careful not to lose the O-ring.

Mounting a Cartridge Housing

1. Determine where the filter is being installed, and install support brackets if necessary.

2. If your pipe system is nonmetal, screw in the two long galvanized (normally ¾-in.) pipe nipples—one into each female threaded end of the cartridge filter head. This gives you a rigid pipe to secure in the support brackets. If the pipe is copper, sweat a male adapter onto a 6-in. copper pipe (you'll want two of these). Screw one into each end of the housing. Place them parallel to the water line, and determine where to cut the copper main line pipe. Mark the pipe for cutting.

3. Turn off the water to the house plumbing and drain the lines. If you have an electric water heater, turn it off, too.

4. If the pipe is being mounted elsewhere, determine how much material is needed to get the pipe to that location. Verify that you have all the pipes and fittings you need before you cut the line.

5. Cut the lines. Have a tub or bucket handy to catch the water that will pour out of the pipes. If the water lines are copper, make the cut at the previously marked location. Install the filter housing using unions or sweat on couplings.

6. Route the pipe to the filter location (if needed) and then connect all plumbing.

7. Double-check all joints, install the cartridge in the filter, turn the filter handle to "on," and turn on the water to the house.

8. Check for leaks.

Replacing the Filter

Turn off the house main shutoff valve, and release the house water system pressure via an outside valve, spigot, or clothes washer. The removal of house pressure makes unscrewing the cartridge filter housing very easy. Normally, I don't even need to use a wrench. Leaving the house water pressure on (and turning the filter unit itself to "off") makes unscrewing the cartridge filter very hard, if not impossible.

1. Turn the filter handle to "off," if it isn't already in that position.

2. Using your hands, a special handle, or a large pipe wrench, unscrew the cartridge housing from the upper base. If it is overhead, turn counter-clockwise. If it is in front of you, pull it toward yourself from the right side of the filter.

3. Water will spill as you remove the housing, and the iron in the water may stain your clothes. Be careful not to lose the O-ring seal.

4. Regrease the O-ring seal with Vaseline or plumber's grease. Put the O-ring back into its groove on the cartridge housing.

5. Insert the new cartridge filter into the housing.

6. Verify that the O-ring seal is in place. Keep the cartridge centered in the housing as you screw the back of the housing onto the upper base. Typically, hand-tightening is sufficient if you are strong. Otherwise, use the special wrench designed for your filter or a large pipe wrench.

7. Turn the filter handle to "on."

8. Turn on the house water. Check for leaks. If there is a major leak, the usual culprit is a lost or damaged O-ring.

WHAT CAN GO WRONG

A slow drip at the female threaded connection into the filter housing. Unless there are unions, this means you have to start all over again.

Installing a Booster Pump

Low water pressure is a common complaint, especially for bathrooms on upper floors. If you live in the city, you may have low pressure coming into the house. If you live in the country, you may have an old pump that can't raise enough pressure or the pump may need to run 20 minutes to get just a couple pounds more. If your pump is not old, you may be able to have a plumber adjust the pressure switch (and then the air in the bladder pressure tank). Whether in the city or the country, many people think they have to live with the problem. Not true. All you have to do is install a booster pump in your basement or crawlspace

For city dwellers, the pump needs to be installed in the main water line just past the main shutoff valve. Country folk install the booster pump where the water comes into the house just before it goes into the pressure tank.

Though most any jet pump will work, I install only the Jacuzzi RP2. It is designed so that the low-pressure water feed goes right into its nose, and you then have several options for places (¾-in. female threads) to take off the high-pressure water. The motor is universal—that is, either 120 volts or 240 volts—and can be replaced without disconnecting any of the plumbing.

In the real-life situation described here, my customer wanted to increase his house water pressure. His water came from another house about 200 ft. away, and by the time it got to his house, he had only 20 lb. to 30 lb. of pressure. We wanted to increase pressure in his house without adversely affecting pressure in the other home, just as a city dweller would want to increase the pressure in his or her house without increasing pressure in the city water lines.

The solution is a booster pump with a check (one-way) valve. The pump takes the low-pressure water coming into the

Adding a Booster Pump

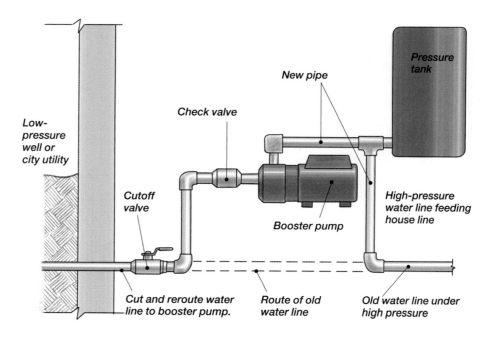

The incoming water line is rerouted to a booster pump input. The high-pressure water is routed from pump output back to the main water line.

Low-pressure well or city utility

Check valve

New pipe

Pressure tank

Cutoff valve

Booster pump

High-pressure water line feeding house line

Cut and reroute water line to booster pump.

Route of old water line

Old water line under high pressure

Booster Pump Installation

Within this pipe, water pressure is only 20 psi to 30 psi. The pipe must be cut and a booster pump installed. The existing water tank is useless (too low water pressure and the bladder is broken).

Prepare the booster pump by screwing in a 1-in. nipple and placing a check valve into the nose (suction end).

Set the pump on blocks so that it is in line with the incoming pipe. The pump output (70 psi) goes to the house with new pressure tank tapped into line. The tank will now pressurize and hold water.

house as its input and builds the water pressure. At the same time, the one-way check valve keeps the pressure from bleeding back through the pump and into the lines. Without the check valve, you would be attempting to pressurize the city water system once the pump turned off. To install the check valve, screw a 1-in. nipple into the pump head. Screw on the check valve. (Be careful not to install the check valve backward; it should open toward the pump head.) Some pump manufacturers have built in the check valve; if so, do not add a second. The incoming water line connects into the check valve.

Boosting Your Hot Water Supply

If you're like me, you like long showers. Turn on the shower, lean back, and let the world go away. The only problem is you run out of hot water all too soon, especially if you use a multihead shower system. To increase the water supply, you can either replace an existing water heater with a larger one or add a second water heater. The latter is always better. Simply add a second water heater *in series* with the first so that the hot output of one feeds into the cold input of another. This will double your shower time. I've hooked up many such systems for large families. Ideally, you want two 52-gal. water heaters in series or parallel.

Why two heaters instead of one real large one? First, if you have a single giant water heater you'll pay for heating all the extra water 24 hours a day. If you have two heaters, you can leave one off most of the time. Turn it on at the circuit breaker 1 hour before the greatest demand, then turn it off when showers or baths are finished. Second, the pur-

chase price of water heaters larger than 52 gal. is very high because few are sold.

If your home is heated using gas, it's best to add an electric heater for the second tank—because the flue won't be large enough for a second gas heater, and it could be expensive and complicated to run a new gas line to the new heater. Install the electric heater as the second in the series, so that the quicker-heating gas heater feeds into it.

To install a new electric water heater, you will need to run cable (or conduit) and install a new 240-volt circuit in your service panel (see my book *Wiring a House* for detailed instructions).

Of course, you can also use a super water-saver showerhead to lengthen shower time. (All showerheads made today are water-saver showerheads.) But this takes away the fun of the waterfalls and rain. The Zoe multi-showerhead unit gives you the option of having two types of showerheads: one a water saver and the other a super water saver.

Installing a Basement Toilet

You could install a basement toilet and sink the hard way—by tearing up the concrete floor and running drain lines. A more practical solution is to buy a kit that pumps the waste away. Installing one is not as difficult as one might imagine. The Zoeller Pump Company makes such a kit. It consists of a rectangular-shaped plastic tank that sits on a concrete basement floor, a sewage pump, and miscellaneous parts. The waste that goes into the tank is ground up and sent out via the sewage pump (located in the back of the tank) through a 2-in. drain line plumbed into an existing overhead 3-in. or 4-in. sewer

Serial Water Heaters

Series-connected water heaters provide a massive amount of hot water over an extended length of time.

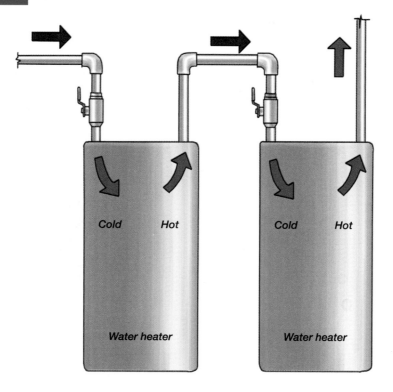

Cold   Hot

Cold   Hot

Water heater

Water heater

Parallel Water Heaters

Parallel water heaters provide a massive amount of hot water in a short length of time.

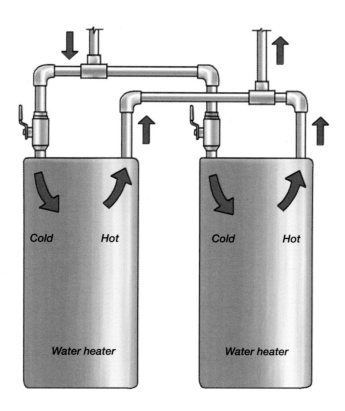

Cold   Hot

Cold   Hot

Water heater

Water heater

The Zoeller kit as it comes, unboxed. Lay out all parts; determine where each goes; and don't, under any circumstances, loose any.

WHAT CAN GO WRONG

You use a 2-in. vent as opposed to the required 3 in. The system will not pump properly.

line. A 3-in. vent must be installed to the tank as well.

The tank has a low end and a tower end—where the drain and vent lines terminate. The toilet sits atop the low end, and the sewage pump sits within the tower. The entire unit can fit in the bathroom, but it's preferable to place the back end of the tank in an adjoining room, to keep ugly pipes from view and to filter out the noise from the pump.

You can mount a common toilet (bought separately) directly onto the tank (the tank is 5½ in. off the floor), but this raises the toilet so high it is a tough climb for kids. I prefer to build a 5½-in. (2x6) wooden frame around the tank with a ¾-in. plywood floor. This gives a normal bowl-to-floor height.

A shower or tub, if wanted, should be installed on a platform immediately adjacent to the tank. Since both have a bottom drain, the platform must be at least 9 in. high so that the shower drain can be pitched downhill to the tank.

Measure carefully if you have a 7-ft. ceiling in the basement. You may find that there is little vertical room for the door or surround of a standing shower. You can trim down a surround, but not a glass door. At least two manufacturers make a neo shower-door (corner-style

shower) with a door and sides that are 66 in. high (most others are 72 in.).

A cabinet-style vanity can sit directly on the basement floor without a platform; its drain is already quite high as it comes out of the cabinet. The same is true of wall-hung and pedestal sinks. However, one might prefer to raise the entire bath floor to have everything at the same height. In this installation, I installed a pedestal sink on the basement floor.

The one question I am always asked about basement toilets with a pump system is: Will there be any sewer smell? The answer, of course, is no, not if the installation is done properly. Another common question concerns toilet paper: Will it collect or be pumped out? The Qwik Jon's model has no problem with accumulation of toilet paper. It has a "free-flow" design, which means a flow is created between plastic floor joists that is evacuated via the sewage pump. The design includes a large ⅜-in. weep hole on the discharge pipe of the pump to aid in waste removal. Be sure to install the pipe so the weep hole points halfway between the left side of the tank (as you stand behind the tower facing the toilet flange hole) and the left plastic floor joist. As the pump kicks on, a strong jet stream from the weep hole blows high-pressure water back into the tank, which rips apart solids and tissue. This creates a fast-flowing river between the two floor joists aided by the suction from the sewage pump.

Installation Tips

■ Read through the directions that come with the kit and be careful not to lose any parts.

■ The tank must rest on a smooth, clean, completely flat floor with no shims. If needed, pour a proper floor under the tank or use sand.

- There is no room for a 2x4 wall between the back of the toilet and tower where the sewage pump sits. Stop the bottom wall plate (the top plate is continuous) on either side of the tank, but continue the finished wall across the front of the tower. This gives you 24 in. plus of finished wall with no vertical stud support. To compensate, install horizontal bracing between the two studs above the tower.

- Build your own 1½-in. shower trap using a flex elbow for the connection to the shower drain pipe. This allows several degrees of flexibility in the hookup and permits a fast disconnect of the shower base. It also allows the drain line to move if the shower base moves slightly up and down as people step in and out of it.

- Use a 1½-in. flex elbow at the shower drain pipe connection into the Y-fitting of the 2-in. drain line that drains into the holding tank. This allows the angle of the shower drainpipe to the Y-fitting to be off by several degrees (left and right or up and down) without any hookup problem and permits fast shower base removal.

- I use 100 percent clear silicone caulk rather than plumber's putty to connect the shower drain to its base.

- I attach the trap and drain assembly to the shower drain and insert all with the shower base. To make this happen, I cut a notch in the wall plate and plywood floor.

- Support the shower drain pipe on the way to the holding tank. Don't leave it hanging in the air.

- To water-test the unit, I run a hose into the shower base, connect a flexible fitting to the 2-in. pipe where it comes out of the tank, and run the 2-in. pipe outside.

- You can adjust the float valve of the sewage pump by raising or lowering the upper stop on the adjustment arm. When assembled, you should have 1 in. of space between the top of the float and the upper stop. You will fine-tune this when you put water in the tank for a test. I had to readjust mine to ¾ in. to get the proper 4½-in. depth of water at the toilet bowl hole for the pump to kick in. The tank holds only 4¾ in. of water at that point, so don't allow the water to go higher than 4½ in. before the pump kicks in (it runs for only a few seconds, anyway). When the pump kicks in, it will lower the water level in the tank to about 3¼ in.

For a fast install, the toilet can sit directly on Zoeller's Qwik Jon tank; but it's a high step for the kids. The wall is optional.

Adding a Basement Toilet

Build a frame around the tank (leaving the back open) and another, higher frame for the shower.

Cut a ⅛-in. "+" shape into the four supplied foam gaskets, and stick the gaskets onto the four offset bolt holes (*arrows*) underneath the steel plate.

Drill four %₃₂-in. holes in the plastic tank at the factory indents around the toilet hole.

Steel Plate Installation

Installation of the steel plate can be a bit tricky.

Step 1

Insert your hand inside the tower and slide the steel plate forward between the plastic joists

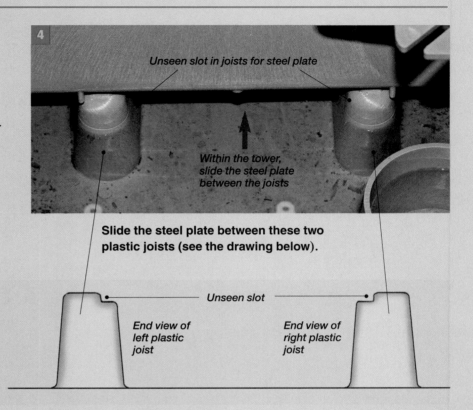

Unseen slot in joists for steel plate

Within the tower, slide the steel plate between the joists

Slide the steel plate between these two plastic joists (see the drawing below).

Unseen slot

End view of left plastic joist

End view of right plastic joist

Step 2

Once the steel plate is under the toilet hole, twist it counterclockwise. The plate will jamb in the slots built into the top of the plastic joists.

Steel plate's off-center bolt slots (with gasket underneath) must align with bolt holes in tank.

Hole in steel plate must be centered directly under toilet hole in tank.

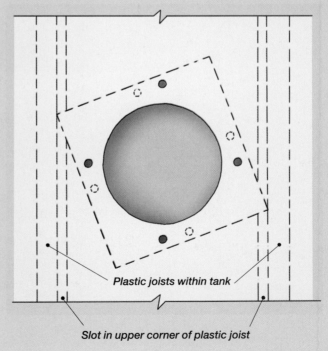

Plastic joists within tank

Slot in upper corner of plastic joist

Adding a Basement Toilet

Insert the supplied bolts through the steel flange and tank holes. Insert the white ring with wax into the tank hole and tighten down with the supplied washers.

Attach the shower drain to the base and install a homemade P-trap system using a flex elbow.

Install ¾-in. plywood over the base assembly, cutting out for the shower drain and pipe and the toilet hole.

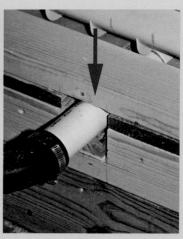

Glue carpet over the plywood. Install the 2-in. drain system from the shower to the holding tank. Though shown here intact (*right*), the plate above the pipe had to be cut in order to remove and install the shower base with drain assembly.

Assemble the switch and float assembly.

Install the seal around the tower lip, insert the supplied 2-in. pipe with the weep hole into pump, set the pump into tower, and install the switch.

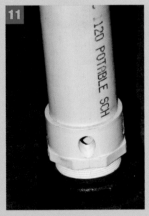

Be sure to point the weep hole between the left side of the tank and first plastic joist.

Locating the Weep Hole

The weep hole in the 2-in. discharge pipe must be angled so the spray direction is halfway between the tank's edge and the plastic joist.

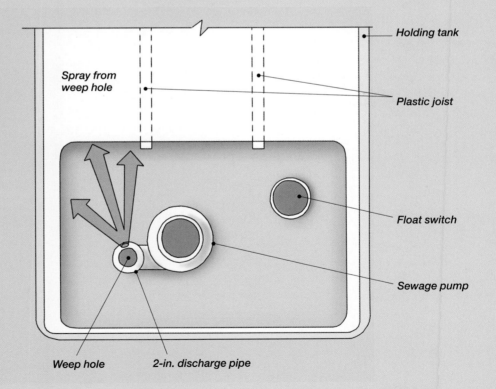

Holding tank

Spray from weep hole

Plastic joist

Float switch

Sewage pump

Weep hole

2-in. discharge pipe

Adding a Basement Toilet

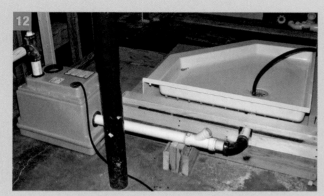

To test the system, I use a hose to fill the holding tank via the shower drain. A flex fitting takes the tank's water outside.

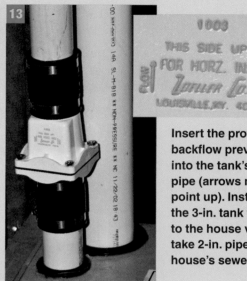

Insert the provided backflow preventer into the tank's 2-in. pipe (arrows must point up). Install the 3-in. tank vent to the house vent; take 2-in. pipe to the house's sewer line.

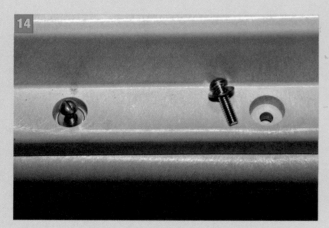

Insert the bolt and washers around the tower base and tighten.

Once the flooring has been laid and the trim is in place and painted, it is time to install the toilet.

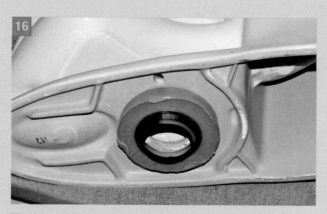

The wax ring can be installed on the toilet horn (as shown here) or on the toilet flange itself.

17 With heavy toilets such as this American Standard Champion, it's best to set the bowl first and add the tank later.

18 Finally, attach the tank to the bowl, and plumb in the water line.

Setup for Holding Tank

Note that there is not enough room between the toilet tank and the holding tank's tower for a full-width stud wall. Terminate the bottom plate on both sides of the tower but continue the finished wall across the gap.

Overhead View

Studs and plate must stop at tower edge of holding tank to allow finished wall to bridge gap.

Studs

Tower end of holding tank

Bottom plate of wall

Finished wall

Optional horizontal bracing between studs to support finished wall

Toilet

Qwik Jon holding tank

CHAPTER 7

Tool Knowledge

TOOLS ARE THE MAINSTAY of the plumbing trade. Particular tools such as wrenches, torches, and tubing cutters were introduced at point of use throughout the book. This chapter focuses on more general information about tools, including problems you might not know, tool designs to avoid, and some basic stuff that never gets discussed.

Having a variety of tubing cutters makes life easier. The round one snaps around the pipe, and the one on the right ratchets.

Pipe Wrenches

You can't do anything in plumbing without a pipe wrench or slip-joint pliers. Whether you are tightening a fitting or pulling one off, a pipe wrench will be needed for either holding or turning. For instance, when you remove a fitting, one wrench will be needed to secure the pipe behind the fitting so it doesn't rotate as you attempt to turn the fitting you want to remove. I normally stock a number of wrenches ranging from 6 in. to 3 ft.

We all know that to tighten you turn clockwise (CW) and to loosen you turn counterclockwise (CCW). But the finer details can be confusing. For instance, should the wrench be facing up or down? And which hand should hold the wrench? The confusion stems from the fact that the teeth of the wrench are angled. If the wrench keeps slipping around the pipe, you have the wrench on backward. Face the wrench in the opposite direction, and it should grab hard.

The teeth on the jaw of a pipe wrench are tapered. Turn this pipe counterclockwise and it will spin. Turn it clockwise and the teeth will grab onto the pipe.

Keep Tools from Disappearing

The problem we all have with tools is that they sometimes disappear on the job.

Painting a tool a wild color can keep someone from swiping it and make it easier to keep track of a tool when someone across the room has it.

Having a home base for tools also helps keep them from being misplaced. I use a common "little red wagon" (borrowed from my grandchild) as a home base. A wheeled wagon is easy to transport from place to place, and once a habit is established for always setting down tools in the wagon (as opposed to a window sill or on the floor), fewer tools disappear. I've never had good luck using the bucket with an apron. Its high center of gravity makes it fall over, and its small circular area means it is hard to find tools and parts within.

To keep from being confused, wedge the "hold" wrench against something (like the floor or ground) with its jaw opening face-up. Tighten a fitting via the left side of your body (by pushing the wrench down), and loosen (as shown) on your right (by pushing down).

■ **WORK SAFE**
■ **WORK SMART**

When you're removing a fitting, the larger the wrench, the easier it will be, because you'll have better leverage.

■ **WORK SAFE**
■ **WORK SMART**

If a fitting appears stuck onto a pipe, heat the fitting with a torch. This will expand the female threads, which will make the loosening easier.

There is a universal pipe wrench (of different lengths) with spring-loaded jaws that can fit several diameters of pipe with no adjustment. I've never felt the need to buy one since common wrenches work so well; thus I can't comment on this tool's effectiveness. It may come into play if you are constantly working with different pipe diameters.

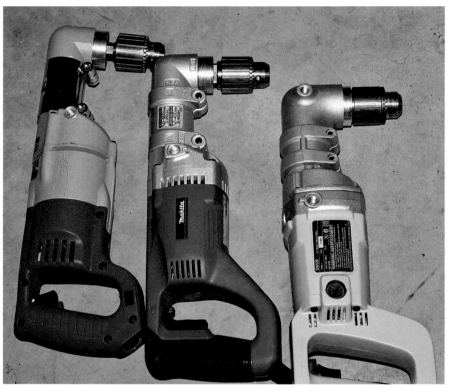

Medium-duty right-angle drills. Not all are created equal.

Right-Angle Drills Can Be Hazardous

All right-angle drills have massive torque and can be dangerous to use. If the bit stalls in the wood, the drill body will start to turn with force sufficient to break the user's arm or jaw. To avoid injury, you would need hair-trigger reflexes to release the drill's trigger as soon as it stalls. As a precaution when using a right-angle drill, brace yourself tight, try to stay off ladders, and always keep body parts out of the way in case the drill body spins.

Right-Angle Drills

When you need to drill a large-diameter hole, you'll want to use a right-angle drill. There are two varieties: heavy duty and medium duty. Stick with the heavy duty. Almost every manufacturer makes a good heavy-duty drill, though this is not true of medium-duty drills.

Avoid a medium-duty drill that has its chuck attached to the drill motor shaft via a small bolt through the center of the chuck. The tiny bolt tends to snap when you reverse the motor—as you would do to extract a stuck bit. A better design uses a keyed system, in which the motor shaft fits into a slot on the chuck to turn the chuck and bit. With this design, the tiny bolt within the chuck can be used to hold the chuck to the motor shaft, but should not be used to transfer the motor rotating torque to the chuck and bit; this is folly, yet is commonly done by a couple of major manufacturers.

Basin Wrench Alternatives

A basin wrench is a long-handled wrench that has a head that turns sideways. It allows you to work under sinks to remove the nuts holding the faucet to the sink and the supply tube to the faucet. Every plumber needs one. However, a basin wrench can be tedious to work with because the spring-loaded jaw doesn't always close tight and the jawed head is often too large to fit in the narrow area between the sink bowl and the wall behind. For such work, you can improvise to create a better tool.

My friend Carl has come up with a grand idea for removing the nuts holding the supply tubes onto the faucet shank.

The tiny bolt that held the chuck onto the motor shaft (and was being used to transfer the motor's reverse torque to the chuck) has snapped (arrow points to jagged broken bolt), allowing the chuck to fall away.

Keyed methods of transferring rotating power from the motor to the chuck are far better than using a single bolt. Makita (*left*) uses a massive amount of metal to extend up into the chuck to turn it. DeWalt (*right*) uses a large cotter pin. Try as I may, I have not been able to snap or even bend the cotter pin. Both designs are great.

Building a Better Mousetrap

Set a flat washer on the pipe, and mark where the wings touch it.

Using a large, flat bastard file, carve down through the pipe (at the marks) about ½ in.

Verify the fit by setting the flat washer onto the pipe.

He uses a specialty automotive wrench, called a claw foot or flare claw foot. This is a 90° open-end wrench head-only that normally fits onto a ⅜-in. socket extension (which would be at a right angle with the extension). He fits the claw foot onto a ⅜-in. ratchet drive handle. He is then able to slide the claw foot under the sink and onto the large nut holding the supply tube onto the faucet's shank, and simply turn the ratchet handle to remove the nut.

Another improvised tool helps remove those flat, circular plastic nuts that hold the faucet shank to the sink. I use a foot-long section of 1¼-in. plastic pipe, and cut a "+" configuration into the end of it. This configuration fits over the plastic nut's wings, and all I have to do is turn the pipe.

Multimeter

Sometimes plumbing work crosses over into the realm of electrical work. When you need to verify voltage, resistance, and continuity, a multimeter is a valuable tool. Choose one that is digital, is auto ranging, and has a large display that is easy to read. A backlight is also helpful when you have to work in dark basements. A good one will cost $50 or more. Avoid cheaper models that are not auto ranging because to use them, you have to switch a knob to an approximate range beforehand. This can be frustrating when you have no idea what the range may be. With an auto ranging multimeter, simply put the meter's leads on the terminals to be measured, and the meter gives you an instant reading.

Cordless Drills

I prefer cordless drills when working on ladders, in crawlspaces, and in wet/damp areas. I've found, however, that they are not all created equal. Here are a few things to watch for:

- Is it easy it is to change the battery? Not all are.
- Does it have an all-metal chuck? The chuck is the mechanism that opens and closes to grab the bit. Plastic chucks crack and break.
- Does it have a chuck lock? I do not recommend any drill that does not have a chuck lock. This is needed to keep the bit from spinning as you install a new one or as you remove an old one.
- Is it easy to change the speed? One drill I tested from a major

Cordless drills with metal chucks are preferred over those with plastic chucks.

WORK **SAFE**
▪ **WORK SMART**

Do not use an extension cord lighter than 14 gauge; it may not be sturdy enough to serve as an extension of the home's wiring; and if it's not, it's a fire hazard.

▪ **WORK SAFE**
▪ **WORK**

When it's important that I drill straight, I sometimes attach a small level to the top of my drill using silicone caulk.

manufacturer had a tiny switch (¼-in. long) to throw for changing speeds. It was very hard to throw and would have been impossible with gloves.

Extension Cords

I only use 12-gauge extension cords because these are sturdy enough to be an extension of the house wiring. For cords over 100 ft. in length, I buy 10-gauge cord by the foot and put my own male and female plugs on. I love cords with lighted ends—it's comforting to know the cord has power as you plug in your tool.

Adjustable Wrenches

You need a number of adjustable wrenches in sizes ranging from tiny to large—not because of leverage, but because of accessibility. Variations in jaw width and handle length add flexibility. Many times, the area where the jaw has to slip on is very narrow. I once had to grind down the sides of a wrench to get it to fit. But you can't grind much. A trick here is to use an end wrench of the required size; you can grind these down all you want. If possible, always opt for adjustable wrenches with wide handles; narrow handles hurt your hand when you really have to put the pressure on.

Levels and Plumb Bobs

I have a collection of several levels ranging from tiny to 8 ft. long. The lengths most commonly used for pipe leveling are 6 in., 2 ft., and 4 ft. Don't forget to put the proper size shim on the level to quickly add a slope of ¼-in. per foot for drain lines. A small level is handy for sections of pipe shorter than 6 in. Long levels are helpful for checking floor joists. Placed at right angles across floor joists, they can span several joists at once to show which are high and which are low. They are also useful to verify that walls are plumb.

Plumb bobs are going the way of the dinosaur but can still be used to find long straight lines or to locate where a plate should go on the basement floor below an existing floor joist. If yours is lost, a chalkline or a string tied to a heavy weight will do. A trick here for finding straight lines from a distance is to hold the plumb bob at arm's length in front of you, then superimpose the line over a house or house frame 60 ft. to 80 ft. away. The line will show you what is straight from footer to roof.

Ladders

Do not use metal ladders unless you have a death wish. Wooden ladders are good but get wobbly after a short time. Fiberglas are best. Possibly my most used ladder (of sorts) is a little Rubbermaid step stool. It's the one everyone keeps trying to swipe. Paint yours a bright color and put your name on it!

Storing Fragile Levels

To protect your level, store it in a section of plastic drainpipe that is slightly longer than the level itself; glue a cap on one end, and a cleanout on the other. Stuff some plastic grocery bags down the pipe to act as a cushion.

Index